ESSAYS

ESSAYS

By

PERCY STICKNEY GRANT

Essay Index Reprint Series

BOOKS FOR LIBRARIES PRESS

FREEPORT, NEW YORK

First Published 1922
Reprinted 1968

PN
710
G65
1968

LIBRARY OF CONGRESS CATALOG CARD NUMBER:
68-22916

PRINTED IN THE UNITED STATES OF AMERICA

TO

JOSEPH S. AUERBACH

MEMBER OF THE NEW YORK BAR
A GENIUS IN HIS PROFESSION
AN IDEALIST WHO KNOWS AND LOVES THE BIBLE
A WONDERFUL FRIEND

Contents

Is Bernard Shaw an Immortal?

ROBERT LOUIS STEVENSON, on his first journey across the United States, was amused by an American fellow-traveler, who inquired his name and his business, but then relapsed into silence, evidently convinced, says Stevenson, "He had plucked out the heart of my mystery." Americans, it may well be, fancy that they easily plumb the human depths. I myself may be about to illustrate this national conceit. So take note that modesty is not encouraged by the companionship of Shaw.

Although (fortunately for you) I am in possession of the key to G. B. S. I do not intend to open many doors. I shall not drag you over the whole establishment, but just glance into a few rooms.

A reactionary criticism, in New York, given a wide audience, inculcates the notion that Shaw is not serious; that he cannot write well constructed plays; that his subjects are too much from the clash of his time to be universal in their appeal and that, consequently, his plays will not last. These are the rooms in Shaw's house-beautiful that I wish to enter.

You may go away from our séance asking yourself a hundred questions (such is the contagion of Shaw's mental activity) a hundred questions which I have not answered. I hope this may be the case. Do not on this account regret your dollars. The power to ask a new question is worth paying for; in addition, as you see, I contract to answer three or four old ones.

Is Bernard Shaw an Immortal? At the age of 60, having been a public person in England for nearly a quarter of a century, Mr. Shaw appears to his fellow-citizens incomprehensible. "The fact is," said a writer in the Century Magazine, just before the war, "Shaw is still a hopeless enigma to the general public, a personal problem, defying solution; an evasive though brilliant intellect that mystifies by striking for and against every subject he discusses."

Even the New Republic had an article by a friendly hand entitled: "Mr. Shaw's Diverted Genius," which contends that genius should stand apart from public affairs and authoritatively issue its special edicts; that it should not jostle with the crowd or rush to the defense of the weak. Mr. Shaw is accused of having fallen into the "habit of mechanically refusing to take things at their face value. Faced with an egg he would impute disingenuousness to the hen." So he sees disingenuousness everywhere, in Viscount Grey and British officialdom.

Before the war an enigma; in war-time a diverted genius. Which would you prefer to be,—a Chinese puzzle or a fish out of water?

The storm of abuse and misconception that beat upon

Shaw in the English press for his strictures on the war during its first months, affords convincing proof that it is one thing to amuse select, even large, theatre audiences and quite another to educate citizens into disciples.

Here in America, whenever Shaw's name is mentioned, there is an invariable question: "Do you really think Shaw is serious?" The counterpart to this query forty years ago was a similar literary puzzling, "Is not Thackeray a cynic?" How odd that Shaw now laughs at Thackeray for being a sentimentalist, just as your children will laugh at Shaw for being too serious, too ascetic, too abstemious, too religious.

But cannot we learn something substantial about our enigma? Who's Who in the Theatre has no room for nonsense. What does it say?

"George Bernard Shaw, dramatic author, born in Dublin, July 26, 1856; son of the late George Carr and Lucinda Shaw; married Charlotte Frances Payne-Townshend; his first play Widowers' Houses was produced at the Royalty Theatre, under the auspices of the Independent Theatre in Dec., 1892. This was followed by the production of Arms and the Man, at the Avenue, April, 1894. During the following ten years his plays were performed chiefly in Germany, America and the provinces, and remained practically unknown in London, except through private subscription performances and through their publication in a more readable form than the old-fashioned acting editions. Mr. Shaw is the author of the following plays: The Man of Destiny, 1897; Candida, 1897; Caesar and Cleopatra, 1899; The Devil's Disciple, 1899; You Never Can Tell, 1900; Captain Brassbound's Conversion, 1900; Mrs. Warren's Profession, 1902; The Admirable Bashville, 1903; John Bull's Other Island, 1904; The Philanderer, 1905; Man and Superman, 1905; How He Lied to Her Husband, 1905; Major Barbara, 1905; The Doctor's Dilemma, 1906; Getting Married, 1908; Press Cuttings, 1909; The Shewing Up of Blanco Posnet, 1909; Misalliance, 1910; The Dark Lady of the Sonnets, 1910; Fanny's First Play, 1911; Overruled, 1912. Of these Mrs. Warren's Profession and The Shewing Up of Blanco Posnet were censored and cannot be publicly performed in Great Britain. In addition, he has written Pygmalion, Great Catherine and Androcles and the Lion. During the Bedrenne-Barker régime at the Court, 1904-6, Mr. Shaw's plays were the predominating features of the enterprise. He was art critic to the World and Truth; was musical critic to the World, the Star and dramatic critic to the Saturday Review. He has written novels, many works on Fabianism and Socialism and on the works of Ibsen and Wagner. His Dramatic Opinions and Essays were reprinted from the Saturday Review in 1907. Is well known as a platform speaker and agitator of social and religious questions; is a member of the Academic Committee, and the Dramatic Committee of the Society of Authors. His plays have been translated and performed all over the continent of Europe and in America, Australia, etc. Address 10 Adelphi Terrace, W. C. Telegraphic address Socialist, Westrand, London."

If you set out to learn something about Shaw from other sources than his plays, you meet, as you see, with difficulties. Who's Who is a death's head caricature, bare of reference to his boyhood and poverty in Dublin and to the struggles of his young manhood in London—that is to say, to the influences which forced his mental development. A colorless, clammy catalogue cannot help us with Shaw.

His biographers, on the other hand, are over-burdened by his many-sidedness. They either pelt him with paradoxes like Chesterton; hail him as a brother-revolutionist like McCabe; treat him with Boswellian minuteness of analysis, plus a moral qualm like Henderson; or worship him like his French biographer, Augustin Hamon.

Shaw's portrait may be drawn without making him a Mephistopheles, or a Moses, or without calling out to him: "Blow, Machiavelli, blow," as some of the haters of his cool self-advertisement might be tempted to do.

His Dublin birth; his going to work at the age of 15; his migration to London at 21; his communistic anarchism and Hyde Park oratory; his hearing Henry George and conversion to single tax; his joining the Fabian Society and writing for it; his plodding throughout his twenties at literary productions which nobody paid for; supported meanwhile on the slenderest fare—vegetarian

[13]

—by his mother's daily sixpence, earned by her music-teaching; his friendship with William Archer, which led to his being given a job at the age of 29 to write art criticism,—later music critiques, then dramatic,—these rather commonplace, if not sordid, conditions are important biological fragments and come near telling his whole story. They come near to plucking the heart out of his mystery.

I know of no author whose life more exactly explains his writing. This was necessarily the case in one unencumbered with university training and tradition, which too often hold the mind back from fresh enthusiasm by their insistence that the classics are the only models for literary form and that history is mere repetition.

If we find Shaw perplexing, why do we ignore his love for autobiography? What can be more explicit than his own confessions and self-explanations?

Much of this misunderstanding about Shaw is prejudice. What the English don't like about him is, at bottom, his race—the Irish always fighting with them and laughing at them. Either the English cannot understand the Irish brand of self-assertion and humor or they loathe it. For the Irishman laughs at everything including himself. Nor do the English comprehend how a man can laugh at himself without being a mountebank. Humor to them is a personal libel; the truer it is the worse it is. The Irish, on the contrary, see themselves as others see them, and appreciate how funny they are.

A Socialist friend of mine—an Orangeman—told me that Socialism did not succeed in Ireland. When the Irish delegates to Socialist conventions met to discuss their theories as a cure for Ireland's ills, they looked into each other's faces and burst out laughing.

The current prejudice against Shaw I, myself, for a long time, shared. I even resented his affront to British dignity.

His prefaces, brilliant but egotistical, to an extent unheard of in English letters, seemed to perform the service of a mirror to G. B. S. in which his vanity could behold his full measure. He not only seized opportunity; he went forth and manufactured occasion for standing in the lime-light. He insulted well-disposed hostesses to be headlined as an unaccountable, incredibly witty and terrible personage. He was a social highwayman who held up his victims for their reputation, for their esprit and left them ridiculously impoverished before the public, with their brains turned inside out, reduced to the mental poverty of fools. His endless public controversy, his pushing and puffing, his naked display of personality, with the vanity, buffoonery and wildness that underlay it—Englishmen could not tolerate nor could anyone else with their prepossessions. Shaw seemed the perpetrator of a continual hoax upon the public, at which he raised his eyebrows in sinister de-

[15]

rision, as it squirmed with resentment and perplexity;—
a revealer of sham infernos, standing by the side of a
trap-door on a stage, when in the end the furious flames
turned out to be nothing but a matter of red fire provided for a gaping audience, to which he furnished its
money's worth of thrills and shocks. Insatiable vanity
wrapped up with insincerity in lectures and laughter—
that seemed to me a good enough formula for Shaw.

The first light that turned me to Shaw was Fanny's
reply to Trotter who had assured her that he went in
for the serious side, short of course of making himself
ridiculous.

Fanny. "What, not make yourself ridiculous for the
sake of a good cause? Oh, Mr. Trotter. That's
vieux jeu."

That reversal of all the English and American dread of
ridicule will carry a man or a woman as far as one
generation needs to go.

Not only did I find myself in the company of a man
who had mastered the most cowardly and stubborn of
fears—the fear of ridicule, but I found him sustaining a
favorite older philosophy of mine, that of the third Earl
of Shaftesbury. Had I not bought Shaftesbury in two
fine old editions because there I found comments upon a
still older voice, Gorgias in Aristotle, crying Shaw's
cry twenty-five hundred years ago: "Seria risu, Risum
Seriis discutere," to Latinize the Greek—which means,
says Shaftesbury, humor is the only test of gravity and

gravity of humor. For a subject which will not bear raillery is suspicious and a jest that cannot bear a serious examination is certainly false wit."

Shaftesbury, two hundred years ago, contended for the free use of humor in religion and went to Greek philosophy for authorities. In Shaw's plays I found in active dramatic battle this further extension of the meaning of humor. His humor was used to religious ends. How much alike, Shaftesbury's philosophy and Shaw's! Hear one then the other. Shaftesbury complains: "But some gentlemen there are so full of the Spirit of Bigotry, and false Zeal, that when they hear Principles examin'd, Sciences and Arts inquir'd into, and Matters of Importance treated with this frankness of Humour, they imagine presently that all professions must fall to the ground, all Establishments come to ruin, and nothing orderly or decent be left standing in the world. They fear, or pretend to fear, that Religion itself will be endangered by this free way, and are therefore as much alarm'd at this liberty in private conversation, and under prudent Management, as if it were grossly used in publick Company or before the Solemest Assembly."*

Now hear Shaw: He calls "Morality the substitution of custom for conscience." "Nowadays we do not seem to know that there is any test of conduct except morality; and the result is that the young had better have their

---

*Shaftesbury Characteristics Wit and Humor, vol. I, p. 74.

souls awakened by disgrace, capture by the police and a month's hard labor than drift along from their cradles to their graves, doing what other people do for no other reason than that other people do it and knowing nothing of good or evil, of courage or cowardice or indeed anything but how to keep hunger and concupiscence and fashionable dressing within the bounds of good taste, except when their excesses can be concealed. "I hate to see dead people walking about; it is unnatural." St. John and Shaftesbury composed that sentence together. "I know thy works that thou hast a name that thou livest and art dead." Sounds from the Book of Revelation, but with humor added. English drama in its early development associated comedy closely with religious symbolism. Roaring farces preceded the moralities.

In short, I found in Shaw's theatre humor playing for the serious side of life according to the best precept of the part. He was in the line of the great seers of truth and the great regenerators of men—not a buffoon but a prophet.

Yes, Shaw is rather exactly fulfilling the rôle of Hebrew prophet. Like his prototype, he declares himself frankly upon personal and political problems without the responsibility of office. He does not have to think of the consistency supposed to exist between pronouncements and platforms or between pulpits and creeds. He disclaims all responsibility for British institutions, except that of criticizing them. An arch-critic in his detachment, he becomes a consummate anarchist, levying upon the state the tribute of attention and conviction.

While everybody in church and state incensed by extremists and their counsels of perfection, proclaims compromise to be the only ideal for the very members of these institutions, Shaw rocks with revolution every organism in which men co-operate with each other. He shakes the ground of past attainment under their feet. He is the extraordinary spectacle of modern democracy —a man challenging the basis of every institution (as much a foe to the state as the early Christians) yet living quietly and comfortably under the law of King George and Mrs. Grundy. An ascetic individualism which in past ages would have retired from the world to enjoy monastic seclusion, and tend a vineyard, rushes as a revolutionary force into modern life to secure to fathers, mothers, children the material and spiritual advantage of Socialism. He is contradiction inherent in the anarchism of chartered criticism and in the freedom of the unfettered prophecy: perhaps more, he is free-speech using its freedom; he is democracy in motion.

You may be tiring of my personal tone—at the slow steps of my pilgrimage to the sage of 10 Adelphi Terrace, W. C., whose telegraphic address is Socialist. You are saying, perhaps, it is all very well for Socialists, heretics, reformers, suffragists, to be charmed by a teaching that lifts them above the power of ridicule which they richly deserve, and should receive—if the jails happen to be full. It is all very well for parsons to find strains from Patmos in Hibernian comedy. But we who sit before you are not too much the friends of these; it is enough that we have to endure a creature who says that marriage is the most licentious of institutions, which is the reason of its popularity. A veritable Pagliacci who proclaims: "Like all dramatists and mimes of genuine vocation, I am a natural born mountebank." "I leave the delicacies of retirement to those who are gentlemen first and literary workmen afterward. The cart and the trumpet for me." What can you say that will reconcile us to this befouler of the home, this street-vendor of his own wares, this self-confessed mountebank?

This is my reply: Why cannot you and I be cured together of prejudice and shocks? I blush to admit that when Candida was first given in America I would not see it because I did not propose to pay Shaw for making a fool of a clergyman. Think what I lost! Are you in any worse plight of ignorant alarm?

How does one get over this antagonism to Shaw? Let us see. I got over it by the discovery that Shaw was putting upon the stage plays which contained more of the fullness and intricacy of modern life than any other playwright. That the world was a bigger and more important place in his theatre than in any other. That here was a man, self-educated, handicapped by the prejudice felt in London against Irishmen, against men without connections or wealth, especially against Socialists and agitators, who made his way up until he stood among the most privileged political and social powers in the world. Shyness, silence, down-heartedness are not the weapons for mortal combat. Self-confidence and self-assertion or nothing must be used. Remember, too, that behind the English character, if we are to believe its greatest native delineators, there is something of the snob and the bully which can only be moved by its own medicine—contempt and challenge. To kick the man below you and to lick the boot of the man above, is the inevitable pliability of a rigid society depending upon an upper privileged class. In Pygmalion, Henry Higgins (the hero) starts out by bullying Liza, the flower-girl, and keeps it up until the curtain goes down. His last chuckle is a blow. He knew that the brute in man rules women of the lower classes; but bullying suited his middle-class nature and methods. Anyone who has seen a booted Englishman in India kick a naked native, is willing to say that Shaw understood how to deal with his adopted countrymen; his blackguard pose of insolent superiority is merely a device for making the punishment fit the crime.

For his higher aerial mastery, Shaw has to manoeuvre his Pegasus to a position above his opponent, from which he can mercilessly attack him. He took a high tone. A wild Irishman and Hyde Park orator plagued duchesses and bewildered the non-conformist conscience. An unplayed dramatist belittled Shakespeare. Shaw seemed to do naturally what Lord Northcliffe expected his staff to do. "To raise hell with everybody." For Shaw to receive attention was to receive encouragement; for him to stir up discussion and counter attacks was to succeed. His attitudinizing was quite self-conscious. "The trumpet and the cart for me." This pose which can be called any name we reserve for self-advertisers; this Grub-street Barnumism shows what it can become when, during the war, we saw one man stand against his own nation, its statesmen, generals, editors, clergy, although they were united and proudly angry from war. Will he be heard? Yes, he is heard. No solitary unofficial pen has dared so much, except perhaps Zola and Hugo and Harden, since Voltaire.

But cannot we take Shaw's word for it that he is serious?

"People talk all this nonsense about my plays because they have been to the theatre so much, that they have lost their sense of the unreality and insincerity of the romantic drama. They take stage human nature for real human nature, whereas, of course, real human nature is the bitterest satire on stage human nature. The result is that when I try to put real human nature on the stage, they think that I am laughing at them. They flatter themselves enormously for I am not thinking of them at all; I am simply writing natural history very carefully and laboriously, and they are expecting something else. I can imagine a Japansee who had ordered a family portrait of himself, and expected it to be in the Japanese convention as to design, being exceedingly annoyed if the artist handed him a photograph however artistic, because it was like him in a natural way. He would accuse the photographer of making fun of him and of having his tongue in his cheek.*

We confound seriousness as an end with seriousness of method, which is quite another thing. The end of life is serious enough; but we do not carry a daily death's head. English puritanism insists that a serious man is serious in all his ways,—serious when he sits down and when he rises up; serious in his tragedy and in his comedy; and that when seriousness ends there he must stop. This long-faced tradition crops out in Emerson's disparagement of laughter and in the failure Mark Twain suffered in his assault upon the Boston literary Olympus. This theory of laughter united in hypocritical union, museums as places of self-improvement with the stage as a place of entertainment. This theory got the Englishman dubbed a man who took his pleasures sadly and what is worse labelled him a Pharisee.

Shaw's formula is: Be sure of your fact, then express it as flippantly as you please. This is only another way of saying that when you present a truth to the world you should make it attractive. This too is nature's

*Archibald Henderson's, George Bernard Shaw, "His Life and Works," p. 411.

way—to dress gaily; to form charmingly or to perfume intoxicatingly what is needed for her fertilities.

Shaw baits his hook with laughter; but he finds this laughter in the depths of thought. In fact, he told his French translator, who demurred humbly at the task imposed upon him, because he was not a humorist, not even a college graduate or much of an author, that the man who could make men think could make them laugh. Shaw's laughter is merely a method of mining thought on deeper levels. The writer who defined a gentleman as a man who left humanity in debt to him, cannot, it is certain, be a mountebank. He is the most serious man of our time because he goes the deepest.

Can Bernard Shaw write a good play? Shaw's plays are objected to by classicists because they are not closely enough woven. Even Henry James, in dissecting play-making, compares it to the scientific packing of a trunk, packed and unpacked until it holds its utmost contents. By others a play is likened to a piece of sound machinery, between the parts of which you cannot insert a knife-blade. But plays can be so tight as to force out the human quality. There must be room for atmosphere between the lines, or the personages seem like manikins.

Play-writing has not maintained fixed characteristics inherited from Aristotle. The three unities, time, place and action are gone. Even the French drama founded upon it has changed. They really went with

[24]

the Greek open-air theatre and its dependence upon the light of day. Shakespeare never observed them. Each age has constructed a drama to please itself; it has omitted some part of the classical recipe and has made innovations. The Greek play-goer ordinarily saw three plays in a day—a trilogy;—a satire, a comedy and a tragedy. Our greatest modern model combines these. Shakespeare was a trust magnate who combined three plays,—comedy, satire and tragedy, in one. Even Hamlet, as originally played, would take now, Ben Greet tells me, seven hours.

What is the sense of talking about a play as if it could be made only in one invariable mould? About every element in play-writing has changed, from plot to the mechanism of character. Soliloquies and asides have disappeared in our own time, which shows us the process.

Architecture has become free, so has painting. Why should not the drama? A few years ago, visitors to impressionist exhibitions exclaimed: "Whoever saw purple shadows? Whoever can call a daub of crude color, spotted like worsted work, a finished picture? Why, when I stand close to it there is no picture at all." The painter has become emancipated, why not the playwright? Mr. Shaw's style notifies us that the drama is emancipated.

Shaw is said not to care for action. His critics say that "action, action, action" is the essence of the drama. If this is so, then it is a coincidence that favors Shaw, that melodrama, the dramatic form that entirely dispenses with ideas in favor of action, has for the present come to the end of its popularity. Moving pictures, it is true, show action but as compared to melodrama they make for realism, richness and thought.

Shaw's critics forget, too, that if you are interested in a thing, it is interesting. Students of modern problems are interested in their illumination, and find it in graphic stage delineations, and in dialogue discussions. In other words, Mr. Shaw's critics fail to do justice to the stimulated and developed mental activity of democracies and their audiences, who "want to know," and find in the theatre their answer.

The masses of the people in our freer countries know well enough their salvation lies in knowledge and will; in ideas organized into social, economical and political advantages. There cannot be a too free or too frequent or too graphic discussion of ideas. In the leading democracy of the world—in France—audiences will listen with delight to good dialogue about great subjects when there is no action at all. The stage is democracy's school.

Shaw chose M. Augustin Hamon, the editor of L'Humanité Nouvelle, to be his French translator, because, as he said, after reading his volume on Le Socialism et le Congrés de London, he was convinced that M. Hamon was the man to make a French translation of his comedies. Mr. Shaw felt sure that if his ideas were understood his comedy would be perceived—that it was not a matter of literature but life; not of expression first but of human relationship, freshly expounded through a new philosophy of life.

Ideas, ideas, ideas, these are what the orator and the actor require today to make them permanently attractive.

At a public meeting in England Mr. Shaw said: "The future of the theatres depended on the drama of ideas. There are three stages of playgoing:

(a) when the Fairy Queen was a real Fairy Queen;

(b) when the actors were known for actors and the scenery for paint and canvas. In this stage the possible combinations were soon exhausted and even the personal fascinations of some particular performer could not make it interesting for long;

(c) when there was a permanent attraction which would compel adults, who had grown out of states (a) and (b) to go on coming to the theatre, and would interest the average respectable man.

These plays would be plays that were 'not plays' but discussions, and should contain as little drama as possible, for drama was only another name for adultery; and passion and adultery were the dullest and most repugnant subjects in the world. Art was no longer Bohemian, and no longer clandestinely opposed to law and custom. The pressure of social bonds was so heavy that the modern endeavor was to find out how to live freely and respectably without breaking the laws; and therein lay the interest and value of the New Drama."

Why ignore or resist ideas until they build Krupp guns to tear you to pieces?

Shaw is trying to turn a stare into a thought; horse-play into the revelation of our inconsistent hypocrisy; eroticism into the clash of ideas. He is a drill-master of stiff brains, which he limbers up by laughter.

Let it pass, then, you cry out, that Shaw is serious; that he has as much right to his style of play as Sophocles had to his. What do you say to his enemies who deny him lasting fame because he uses passing subjects?

Will Shaw's plays last? This question involves the make-up of comedy. If its function is what Meredith assigns: "Nothing less than the destruction of old established morals," then it is bound to be less acceptable to later ages than our own. The shock of the inconsistent which excites laughter when the writer of comedy excoriates his contemporaries, is turned into faint surprise towards some historic phase of social backwardness, when the old comedy is revived.

I am always disappointed in dramatic revivals. Where has the magic of the old piece gone? I admire the mastery of materials, but even an all star cast cannot restore the glamor of a revival. Wit is perpetually breaking the shell of ignorance to present new life; but when at last you have the life, wit's task is done and its voice sounds hollow. So in old comedy there is great loss from evaporation.

How much of Shakespeare's fun has evaporated we shall never know. To me most of it is gone. His horse-play for the apprentice, his punning (once a courtly humor), his social satire have lost their meaning and their flavor. His chief comic character, Falstaff, is beaten a hundred times by Sienkiewicz's Zagloba.

The mechanical playwright flatters himself that he is dealing with universal human nature when he avoids fads and contemporary public controversies. But the great writers of comedy have not satirized human nature as if it were a stationary thing, but human nature under conditions peculiar to the times, and living personalities who amused them. Aristophanes got his fun out of Socrates and the Sophists; Plautus out of the life of his day, out of masters and slaves, etc.; Molière out of the clash of old and new and out of pretentious groups; Brieux out of the terrifying new social enlightenment that science is disclosing; Shaw, out of the three-class system in England, and the dilemma of stranded creeds in an age of transition.

Molière's theatre was the comedy of contemporary social satire. He was as up to date in his shafts as Gilbert, yet great voices in his time—for instance—Corneille—denied him merit except as a farceur. Literary affectation or theatrical pretence, are no more a universal trait than social, religious, philanthropic, dramatic—in fact all manner of pretence.

[29]

Because Wagner burlesqued the minnesinger is the Meistersinger less of a masterpiece?

No. Shaw does not suffer with posterity because his subjects are larger than the average English comedy displays.

Nietzsche said the Germans had no culture, as was shown by their destitution of style. For style and culture he turned to the French. We all turn to the French for the discovery and perpetuation of beauty. Gallic approval confers immortality without the formality of election to Academy. To Byron and Poe, for instance, France gave an international place and reversed the estimates of their own countrymen. So it is with Shaw. He pleases the French with his comedy of ideas. They love ideas and lead the world in applying them to life. They take ideas seriously, even though taught by laughter. The wittiest people are not accidentally the most hospitable to new thoughts, plastic to its social transformation and devoted to ever-changing, beautiful expression—that is, to style.

The French stage not only tolerates but enjoys discussions—living dialogues. But the living dialogue will demand enough action to carry it, which will be as much as it requires to be absorbed.

In France Shaw's name is coupled with Molière. He is called the Molière of the Twentieth Century. He is further assured by his French biographer that in France the destiny of his plays is to become popular and classical.

Pour votre théâtre, le destin, c'est de devenir populaire et classique en France.

I have answered the questions: Is Shaw serious by saying yes, as serious as possible. Can Shaw write good plays? Yes. His theatre is today more throbbing with life than any other.

Does Shaw's election of contemporary subjects limit his fame? No. All the great writers of comedy took contemporary subjects (unless they were merely adaptors or translators).

Do his blemishes of workmanship or of form hurt him? Not necessarily. Horace accused Plautus of being clumsy in construction and faulty in the drawing of character; yet Plautus' comedies were popular for generations after his death and today college boys, to know their classics, have to read him.

Will Shaw's plays last? Yes, because he has put one of the most active brains of our times to the portrayal of the life of our time. He will be found our greatest portrait painter of men and manners.

After all, what is literary immortality? It is only the lasting longer than your contemporaries; it is not endless fame. Civilizations decay; libraries are burned down; men's minds find vast new fields to feed them and new liberties for which to struggle. Only a few great writers survive their civilization. Shaw stands a chance of such survival because he is a herald of the new. He and Macaulay's New Zealander are already good friends

—the one preaches what the other will codify into law. Possibly it will be Shaw who shows the New Zealander around London. If his visit is long delayed the New Zealander may well make a pilgrimage as to a shrine to the house of the man whose telegraphic address is Socialist, Westrand, London.

Browning's Art in Monologue

THE most splendid tomb in the world is the Taj Mahal, erected by a Mogul emperor as the burial-place of his favorite wife. Made wholly of white marble, which in India retains the quarried brilliancy, it is even more magnificent than Milan cathedral and is properly considered the perfection of Indian Architecture. A noble gateway admits the visitor to a carriage-path running between low, Moorish arched buildings, at the end of which rises a second gateway surmounted by little domes, by itself beautiful enough to be a memorable monument. Continuing along a marble pavement through tropical foliage, one sees ahead the dome of the Taj resting apparently upon dense verdure. At length a succession of marble terraces leads to a platform upon which the whole structure rests. Within the temple, beneath the dome, is a circular marble screen carved in delicate tracery and studded with colored gems. Enclosed by the screen is a sarcophagus on which is cut an inscription in Arabic. The name of the lady buried here is Moomtez-i-Mahal.

It is not due only to the fascination of the Oriental picture, I hope, that in it I see a helpful image of the poetic edifice raised by Robert Browning. The reader passes through the gateway of "Paracelsus," sees a few poems on his way to the second gateway, "Sordello," then treads a path flagged with dramas and lyrics until he reached a great structure, "The Ring and the Book," in which is enshrined "Pompila," the poet's loveliest creation.

Browning was a prolific writer. His admirers likewise have become prolific writers. He has been treated like a science and studied in monographs. The poet and his commentators alone have produced a library, and this bulk is constantly receiving accessions. Any addition is valuable as it is small and deals with well defined sides of the subject.

So let us turn to a neglected corner and attempt a short study of Browning's art in monologue. The form rather than the substance of his poetry will be our concern; the growth of the poet's mastery over his material. Browning's technique ought especially to repay investigation because his style, more than his matter, discourages readers who open his pages for the first time. If they understand his style they understand him. But not only is the style the man, but the man makes the style. His temperament, his times, his topics create the uniqueness of his signature. These we shall have a look at as well is the surface glaze of his work.

A 20th Century lover of poetry cannot imagine the amount of ridicule heaped upon Browning even during the last and popular years of his life,—the number of clever parodies concocted to jeer at his jolting meter; the multitude of jests manufactured to measure the darkness of his meaning. Even Browning himself came to enjoy this satirical literature. Of these shafts one fetched from America by Louise Chandler Moulton he received with uproarious laughter. A Chicago woman, so ran the newspaper item, was entering Boston by rail. As the train drew near the Hub she heard a mighty humming. Upon asking what the strange noise was, the negro Pullman porter informed her, quite casually, that the sound proceeded from the Boston Browning societies, conning the meaning of their master's verse.

A young man who came to his majority in 1833, as did Browning, found himself the citizen of a new world. The end of the old Era is roughly marked by Matthew Arnold at the death of Scott in 1832. Then finally perished the fears of "The Terror"—and likewise the dread, of parting with mediaeval views and institutions; fears aroused by the French revolution and by its Master Napoleon. These fears had led even in England to the persecutions of revolutionary utterances, and to the virtual exile of its great revolutionary voices in literature, Byron and Shelley. But by 1832 even the reactionary compact with Rome (made after Waterloo) by which her conservative offices were sought by Europe was undone. The economic distress, too, that followed the Treaty of Vienna had finally been overcome.

The revolution from mediaeval ideas to modern is well

marked by the death of Scott. New conditions, new problems, new ideas tumbled out upon England almost as suddenly as if let out of a box. The new industrialism of steam and capitalism called even louder than the French peasant voice for democracy and a new personal justice. The Revolution again broke out and made of the 30's one of the most striking decades in history.

In 1833, the year of Browning's first literary venture, Newman joined the Oxford Movement and began the Tracts for the Times that fought on English soil for dying Mediaevalism. In 1836 Darwin in his garden in Kent began the series of experiments which finally found explanation in his volume "The Origin of Species." In 1837 Carlyle wrote the "French Revolution" and brought a new philosophic and literary faculty to bear on the problems of history. In the same wonderful decade Macaulay, Disraeli and Gladstone were young men and moving forces in English political life.

The new industrial factors of the Nineteenth Century were not only the occasion in England of political reforms but of new moralities. Factory legislation was agitated by the Earl of Shaftesbury in 1829. The Reform Bills of 1832 were the results of new industrial conditions and consequent responsibilities.

The difference between the new era and the old is illustrated in English Prison Reform. A man could be hung in England as late as 1818 for stealing four shillings and for nearly two hundred so-called crimes. From

1832 for a dozen years only four suffered capital punishment except for murder.

The surmise, then, of a new scientific attitude, such as afterwards clarified in the theory of evolution, gave substance to speculation. The development of the historical method gave new importance to documents and fact. Philosophy lifted the utilitarian and ethical into paramount importance.

Browning in early life was used to a free religious atmosphere. His parents were at first dissenters but later attended Anglican services. No religious compulsions seem to have been put upon him. The youth who read through Voltaire in his teens, the admirer of Shelley (the anarchist expelled from Oxford for writing the Necessity of Atheism, the year before Browning's birth), the pupil who made Byron his poetic model, was not likely to be found on the side of conventional religious thought, or, for example, to run into the *cul de sac* of sacramentalism and authority that buried Newman.

A wider divergence could not easily be found than the thought of Browning and Newman. Young Newman brought up on Calvin and his dualism of spirit and matter ended his career in Birmingham Oratory, not only unutilized by the church of his adoption, but distrusted. The poet illuminated the relation of spirit to matter, of flesh to soul, in a brilliant gallery of poetic portraits such as had not been dared before.

The ladies who comprised the Browning Societies of

[37]

the last thirty years did not realize that their idol went to school to Voltaire, Byron and Shelley. They probably had never read a word of Voltaire and would not as being the arch-atheist; not much of Byron, as being the arch-traitor to England's morality, and little of Shelley as combining the religious and ethical improprieties of both the others. But from Browning his disciples absorbed the teachings of all the revolutionists, a new theology and a new ethical freedom. This was Browning's extraordinary contribution to the national English interest in standardized moralities.

The ethical dominated the interests of Browning's contemporaries. What mattered art and science except as they helped mankind live? To contemplate, even to create beauty, did not satisfy Browning's generation. Everything must be turned to account. "How to live," as Herbert Spencer put it, "that is the essential question for us." The ethical dominated educational ideals. The Nineteenth Century was preparing for the Twentieth Century efficiency. Matthew Arnold's dictum that three-fourths of life is conduct, was preparing for American sociologist's laudation of action; "Knowledge is vital only when it is transformed into arterial sustenance for action."*

All the great Englishmen of the last century accepted chairs of ethics, and agreed from some point or other to lecture upon conduct. Social philosophers like Spencer, novelists who moralized like Thackeray and George

*Prof. Small, Journal of Sociology.

[38]

Eliot, poets who preached like Wordsworth, were representative of their era. And of course Carlyle. There is a look of the wrinkled brow, of the problem unsolved, of the burden increasing, in short, of moral responsibility, about the mighty men of the Nineteenth Century, which cannot be paralleled in the two previous centuries. To this troubled aspect Browning was an exception. He saw more clearly, he led a broader life, more international, more social, more sane; yet he too was a preacher.

The new era into which Browning was born had another characteristic which the date of Scott's death marks with personal emphasis; it went over from poetry to fiction, just as Scott himself did, as its preferred and popular literary form. Browning shows, as does no other Nineteenth Century poet, the effect of competing fiction. He met prose competition by modifying poetry. He labored to give his lines animation and vivacity, quite after the conversational method of the novel. The preacher's habits and prose writer's tricks he utilized. He brought over the animation of prose fiction into poetry to meet the demand for greater conversational intimacy between the author and the reader. You can feel too as you read him the pounding of the pulpit to wake up the drowsy.

In a generation that so largely cast off poetry in favor of prose fiction; in the reign, in fact, of Dickens and Thackeray, Browning still was devoted to the Muses.

But he brought to their service a new audacity of attitude—a new boldness of the eye; a self-conscious, even egotistical technique coupled with more daring moralization than had yet appeared in English verse. He borrowed from prose a new realism and ad hominem address; he freed poetic beauty from prettiness and used imagination for deeper human analysis. He responded markedly to those demands which produced modern prose fiction.

Another interesting light upon Browning's style is afforded by the special form he selected. In the thirties soliloquy, although in Victor Hugo's dramas it had been carried far, was in a way to be dropped and later was dropped from dramatic devices. Browning picked up this discarded stage ornament and made it the "Captain jewel of his carcanet." Byron already had made a hit with the "Prisoner of Chillon" and "Mazeppa" by means of the directness, force and clearness of monologue. In this mould of the monologue Browning casts his important work. It was the basis of his style and established its personal conversational note; it was the unit of his art by which all that he did can be measured.

Browning's place among English poets is not marked by what some critics consider unaccountable personal peculiarities of workmanship. He was an orderly appearance in English letters. An English poet's Almanac for 1829 could have prognosticated such a career. By taking into consideration the course of English verse, and by understanding the intellectual content of the period, it could have printed: "At this time look out for Robert Browning."

I have never seen Browning's relation to the literary movement of his time carefully studied, nor his debt to his predecessors in England, Byron and Shelley, and to Hugo his contemporary in France, followed up, nor his place in English versification traced.

English verse may be said to start for modern readers with the Elizabethans and to have two main directions. One of these followed the Greek and Latin epics and their Italian imitations, but exchanged the classical hexameter for the ten-syllable line and thus created the blank verse of the Elizabethan dramatists and Milton. The other copied Italian stanzas and produced the English sonnet, ottava rima and the Spenserian stanzas.

The single blank verse of five feet ending with the line, soon gave place to a more pliable unit of versification—a sentence composed of several such verses or parts of verses, balanced and cadenced, but without rhyme. This lengthening of the run of the single line afforded flexibility and room for even Miltonic melody; but in heavy hands became clumsy and tedious. So English poetry tried next for pithiness and neatness, and found these qualities in the couplets of Dryden and Pope, which speedily superseded blank verse. But after a century of heroic couplets, this polished form seemed too mechanical and superficial for the taste of the revolutionary decade of the Eighteenth Century which returned to simpler expression and again to blank verse, but of a sort that lacked Elizabethan and Miltonian grandeur, and wanting, too, their interior melodies, ran monotonously into interminable narrative, as in Wordsworth's Task and the Excursion.

The second development of Elizabethan verse is more Italian than classical. The Italian sonnet became a familiar and honored English form. Italian stanzas are used by Spenser, Byron, Keats and Shelley, but with little expansion of their metrical possibilities. Swinburne was the great experimenter and perfecter of our more intricate and sumptuous Italian tradition which, in his time, became enriched with French forms and animated by French esprit, while astonishingly expanded by a glorious inspiration from Greek dramatic choruses.

Nineteenth Century English poetry, it then appears, has contributed two highly developed studies in the two directions characteristic of our poetry—the narrative and the lyric; the Latin tradition and the Italian tradition. The technical story of Victorian verse could omit every other name except Browning and Swinburne and yet be complete. Tennyson, Arnold, Longfellow added nothing novel to English Prosody.

Browning was the inventor of a new dash and freshness in blank verse. At first he used the same ambling, contemplative lines as his contemporaries until criticism and experience led him to desire terseness and color.

Instead of repeating the Seventeenth Century solution for this problem and using couplets, he tried to preserve the flow and naturalness of unrhymed long lines, but to secure the desired compactness by a conversational style, by omissions, which took much for granted and so left much unsaid; in short, by explosive and abrupt rhetorical figures that effected his purpose, but unfortunately, rendered him difficult to understand. He also used extraordinary rhymes. I repeat, Browning is a more significant figure in the History of English poetry than any of his contemporaries except Swinburne. His style is not a sport on the flourishing tree of English poetry, it is a branch.

As a literary craftsman, then, Browning did several interesting things. He pulled English blank verse out of the contemplative, descriptive, quiet ruts of the Eighteenth Century. He brought into poetry the modern habit of personal comment and made an habitual manner of Byron's frequent pose. Finally, Browning picked out a tid-bit, monologue, from the old drama and made that the *pièce de résistance* of his art.

Many of the spiritual benefactors of the Nineteenth Century—Thackeray, Dickens, Newman, Carlyle, George Eliot, Charles Kingsley, Emerson—had a talent for verse that under Good Queen Bess might have blossomed and become their sufficient medium. But they believed that they could, on the whole, best help their time by addressing it in prose. Browning settled the question differently. He understood his day and generation, but in his constitution imagination and reason were both so strong that his thought expressed itself best in ornate art. He is well aware of the difficulties in his way, and he offers arguments for his choice.

"Why take the artistic way to prove so much?
  Because it is the glory and good of Art
  That Art remains the one way possible
  Of speaking truth, to mouths like mine, at least."

In days, too, when the largest financial return from the pen went to novelists, whose profits per volume are proud items in their biographies, Browning ventured boldly upon a career in which to the end he was to lose money. He ran counter to his time and to its habit of commercial valuations. He plied the poet's trade in a hard market.

The modern poet has a labor which the Greek poets were unburdened by. If the final object of poetry, in our deepest use of it, is the cleansing and lifting of the soul ("Only that is poetry," says Emerson, "which cleanses and mans me"), then the poet must eke out the spiritual inertia of his audience, and attach to his revelation of beauty an index-finger pointing to the absolute. In short, he must interpret beauty in easy ethical terms. A modern artist has to affix a tag to his work to explain it. An example is Keats' "Ode on a Grecian Urn." Four stanzas of the ode reproduce the beauty of the exquisite shape, and it has rarely happened that one art has been so magically transcribed into the symbols of another. Finally, as though he heard the age saying, "Yes, very beautiful, but what of it?" he writes a fifth stanza and thus attaches a card to the urn to announce the moral truth contained in the beautiful form:

"Thou shalt remain in midst of other woe
That ours, a friend to man, to whom thou sayst
'Beauty is truth, truth beauty,' that is all
Ye know on earth, and all ye need to know."

A modern poet who represents his age, cannot be classic in the Greek sense, he cannot present truth free from the accidental; he must be ornate, overlaying the truth to be revealed with analogies and suggestive comments. Such characteristics in our art are encouraged, too, by the greater complexity of modern ideas and life. Our artist is half preacher, he objectifies a truth then dogmatizes it. He does something and explains what he has done all in one work. How this second or explanatory function is to be added to the first or the universal, is the problem of our art. This was Browning's problem, his answer was necessarily a composite art. You feel about it as you do when the mystic lines of a Gothic Cathedral are interrupted by a carved animal form—the eruption violently of ideas and propagandas frankly into the realm of pure art.

Browning treated 19th Century theology in monologue. Milton discussed 17th Century theology and problems of government in epic poems. The monologue was probably derived from the messenger speeches of the Greek drama and has its own modern history, but it was developed by Browning into a form with a distinct range, like the epic, the drama or the lyric. Although Browning has written plays in which he has been truer to classic definitions than most English poets, they were not, in their formal requirements, congenial to his genius. The 19th Century poet, as has been seen, had to give a running commentary on the truth his verse embodies. He had to over illustrate his fact to make it clear to minds not so severely trained to beauty as the Greek. In modern or ancient drama, since the main interest is in the action, any commentary or ornament obscures the movement of the plot. Even in Shakespeare—a profusion of imagery hinders the progress of events. The drama, on this account, was not the best medium for Browning. His monologues are often so dramatic in expression that they persuade the reader he is in the hands of a born dramatist, but upon investigation, the speaker in the poem is always found to be Browning under different names, and the quality of the verse to be not dramatic but contemplative and didactic.

Browning experimented to find a form of poetry in which action and description would exist most happily side by side. His work as an artist has been to discover and develop the possibilities in monologue. Examined from the standpoint of the monologue, all that he has done discloses unity. In "Paracelsus" and "Sordello" he was experimenting with his materials. In "The Ring and the Book" he mastered them. The steps in Browning's art can be easily traced in these three poems.

Quite in the spirit of Browning, I attach, perhaps, undue importance to my figure of the Taj with its two gateways. Still, we may as well keep it in mind while we examine the poet's masterpiece where Pompilia rests, and the two earlier poems, in workmanship tentative and introductory—Paracelsus and Sordello. Yet after asking you to accept my image I must risk marring it, for "Paracelsus" is not Browning's first poem, nor is it to the eye a monologue. However, no harm is done to our first gateway, at most it is given a double arch.

"Pauline," the first weak child of our poet's Muse, was exposed upon the barren hillside of public neglect. It was rescued and deposited in the British Museum. An accident—an American writer's discovery of the volume—compelled its author, late in life, to acknowledge it.

"Paracelsus," which takes pretty much the same subject, is counted as his first work by the poet, and is accepted as such by the public. I must acknowledge that while a page of "Paracelsus" looks like a dialogue it is not. There are a number of speakers—Festus, Aprile, Michal—who give their Master an occasional breathing-space, or jog his memory. So when we start upon a study of Browning's art in monologue with

[47]

"Paracelsus," we are probably doing what the author would wish. Still, a few points in the style of both poems are more easily studied in the earlier one, where a less finished art fails to hide the mechanism.

"Pauline", a fragment of a confession, is a monologue of about a thousand lines in blank verse. The speaker, at the point of death and presumably young, talks to Pauline, the woman he loves. He reviews his life, discusses points in his development, and the causes of his mistakes. The trouble seems to be that he has been pulled in opposite directions.

> "I would have one joy
> But one in life, so it were wholly mine,
> One rapture all my soul could fill."

On the other hand, wisdom attracts him.

> "This restlessness of passion meets in me
> A craving after knowledge * * *
> The sleepless harpy with just budding wings."

His passion is a variation of the choice of Hercules, Venus contending with Minerva for the possession of a soul. He vacillates, and in his weakness secures the help of neither goddess. We encounter him sick, recumbent, talking to Pauline. The picture might as well be Fanny Brawne come to the lonely room in Rome where Keats lay in his fatal illness. At last, she listens and perhaps weeps, as the poet tells over the short bead-roll of his years, and for the last time pours out his soul to a woman.

The influence of Keats, indeed, is plainly perceptible in "Pauline"; but there is also an intellectual element, a disposition to weigh the value of things wholly alien to Keats. The thoughtful vein in the poem reminds one of Shelley, and "Alastor" both in form and spirit may easily have been the father of Browning's first poetic child. Browning admired Shelley most of modern poets, and the following lines in the poem we are examining no doubt refer to him:—

> "And my choice fell
> Not so much on a system as a man—
> One whom praise of mind shall not offend,
> Who was as calm as beauty, being such
> Unto mankind as thou to me, Pauline."

Although life has perplexed Pauline's lover, and he has not known which to choose, beauty or knowledge, at last, by the light of love, he sees more clearly,—

> "For I * * *
> Shall doubt not many another bliss awaits.
>
> * * * * *
>
> As I again go o'er the tracts of thought
>
> * * * * *
>
> And beauteous shapes will come for me to seize,
> And unknown secrets shall be trusted me
> Which were denied the waverer."

In "Pauline," Browning is not as yet self-centered; there are too many evidences of contemporary influence; he is struggling toward maturity and independence, but does not reach his poetic majority until "Paracelsus." The scene of "the confession" he neglects to fix, which shows how early in his career he despised what did not to his mind help the reader's study of a soul—a vagueness easily forgiven a young admirer of Shelley. The opening lines, however, disclose the double poetic allegiance, for they are quite in the style of Keats:—

"Pauline, mine own, bend o'er me—thy soft breast
Shall pant to mine—bend o'er me—thy sweet eyes
And loosened hair," etc.

But the glow of sensuousness in the beginning of the poem soon pales away into cold, intellectual talk about beauty and knowledge.

Browning was aware of his tendency toward cold monotony, and tried to lighten the reader's burden by introducing two episodes; one a description of Andromeda and the dragon; the other a picture of an ideal abode for lovers, like Claude Melnott's improvisation. To help the verse bear off more trippingly a subject that inclined to meditative slowness, he interjected frequent epigrams. More lines in "Pauline" look as if framed to be quoted than in all the rest of Browning's poetry. Most of these ornaments are short, a line or two, I will venture to quote one rather longer than the rest. Autumn stands before us as she might look in a painting by Rossetti.

"Autumn has come like spring returned to us,
  Won from her girlishness, like one returned
  A friend that was a lover, nor forgets
  The first warm love, but full of sober thoughts
  Of fading years, whose soft mouth quivers yet
  With the old smile, but yet so changed and still!"

In the later works there is almost an entire absence of passages that lend themselves readily to quotation. A good thought or a happy analogy is left to take care of itself, and is not helped by roundness of period or grammatical construction, to stand out brighter than its fellows. The choicest passages in Browning begin and end anywhere in a line, and fall in any person, number or tense. Instead of being easily detached they are embedded well-nigh inextricably in the whole. Browning is a hard poet for calendar makers. But we must turn to the second arch of our first gateway.

"Paracelsus" consists of some four thousand lines of blank-verse, broken by a number of songs. In form a dialogue between Paracelsus, Festus, Aprile, and Michal, it is really a monologue. Says the author:

"It is an attempt, probably more novel than happy, to reverse the method usually adopted by writers whose aim it is to set forth any phenomena of the mind or the passions by the operation of persons and events, and that instead of having recourse to an external machinery of incidents to create and evolve the crisis I desire to produce, I have ventured to display somewhat intimately the mood itself in its rise and progress, and have suffered the agency by which it is influenced and determined to be generally discernible in its effects alone, and subordinate throughout, if not altogether excluded, and this for a reason. I have endeavored to write a poem, not a drama."

The poem opens in the year 1512 A.D. From that date onward, the friends meet four or five times before the close of the half century, and on these occasions, Paracelsus narrates what has befallen him. These monologues, with occasional interruptions from the others, constitute the scenes.

Paracelsus is ambitious to grasp all knowledge and to glorify God by shining upon men like a star of wisdom. Every pleasure, every reward of praise or of love, he pushes aside, his goal alone can attract him. He despises praise and lets men see that he can do without it. They in turn hate him. When he laughs at their enmity, they denounce him.

But they were right and he was wrong. He thought them contemptible creatures only because he had no real sympathy for them. When they, deaf to his cold, loveless visions, forsake him, he stoops to conquer, and exchanges for the persuasions of wisdom the terrors of magic. The populace sees through his tricks, resents his appeal to their passions and superstitions, then thrusts him out—a discredited charlatan.

Paracelsus learned that knowledge, to influence his fellow men, must go hand in hand with love. He learned too that a soul must follow its own enlightenment, and, whether it win or lose must not turn to the dark gods of force or fraud. Aprile, a poet, represents the voice of love, which throughout life called constantly to Paracelsus, but to which he was deaf. Festus stands for faith in Paracelsus, but Paracelsus lost faith in himself. At last, however, he sees what a mistake has been made, and with his last breath whispers:

> "Festus, let my hand
> This hand, lie in your own, my own true friend!
> Aprile! hand in hand with you, Aprile!
> *Festus.* And this was Paracelsus."

The author did right to define a work as a poem which on the outside looked like a drama. "Paracelsus" cannot be acted because it has no action. Its force is best felt in reading, but it is hard reading. No one knows whether the experience of Paracelsus represents the soul's growth aright until he himself has passed through similar experiences. To one who has passed through like crises, the poem is a twice-told tale, he knows the story and its lesson. To one who has not lived such a life, the crises are either barely intelligible—that is, as necessary steps in a soul's development—or in comparison with action, they are but mildly interesting. The wisdom of the whole could be contained in half a dozen sonnets, and in that form would stand a much better chance than at present of becoming widely known. Throughout a poem as long as all of the Ovid, we used to read for college, it is a labor to keep in mind the intermediate steps of progress from knowing to loving—a capital sonnet-sequence.

There is no personal attraction about any of the characters. Aprile comes in with a catching verse; but he is too much of an abstraction to interest us. The intangible substance of the poem, points to the radical defect in a species of verse that describes the soul without reference to the body. It is neither objective nor subjective. Held up to nature it is monstrous egotism. Suppose Browning were wrong about Paracelsus, or better, that a soul does not have to develop in the way his hero does, then we are left with nothing—neither the living, acting person of the drama, whose character good or bad, we unravel from his deeds, nor the subjective experience of Browning himself when on some occasion he has received a powerful emotion.

Besides its too great length and its shadowy characters, little more than personifications, there is another fault in "Paracelsus," the same we saw in "Pauline"—lack of warmth and of movement. Towards the end of the poem, there is a need of cumulative effect, but no action is to be got out of such shades as Paracelsus and Festus.

The poet, therefore, permits Paracelsus, when somewhat delirious, to describe the doings of his uncontrolled brain. The result is striking but weak and out of keeping with the rest.

A few songs break the monotony of this long poem, and had Browning done nothing else, they would give him a place in English anthology. Browning's verse is supposed to be rough and ragged, even if like the weapon of Zeus, it be powerful. The following lines breathe the sweetness of the Elizabethan lyrics:

"Heap cassia, sandal-buds and stripes
    Of labdanum and aloe-balls,
Smeared with dull nard an Indian wipes
    From out her hair, such balsam falls
    Down seaside mountain pedestals,
From tree-tops where tired winds are fain,
Spent with the vast and howling main,
To treasure half their island-gain.

"And strew faint sweetness from some old
    Egyptian's fine worm-eaten shroud
Which breaks to dust when once unrolled,
    Or shredded perfume like a cloud
    From closet long to quiet vowed,
With mothed and dropping arras hung,
Mouldering her lute and books among
As when a queen, long dead, was young."

The second gateway in our approach to Browning's masterpiece is "Sordello," an historical poem of about six thousand lines, in five-measure iambic feet with couplet rhymes. In a thirteenth century troubadour, Browning found a type of the artist who, with great natural gifts and the ambition to put knowledge as well as emotion into his work, is confused by the events of life, and dies without accomplishment.

The early sensuousness of Sordello turns into seriousness, and his audience deserts him. He is not self-centered enough to work out for himself a form of self expression in spite of circumstances, but he is controlled by the environment of his age. The Guelf and Ghibelline wars are transforming Italian cities into shambles. Sordello is stirred to action by his keen sympathy with the people, and espouses their side, but he loses his own identity when he exchanges the pen for the sword. His power is dissipated, and his slight accomplishment amounts to failure.

Although incapable of successful action, his will is unshaken. When he discovers himself to be the son of Salinguerra, the most famous Ghibelline soldier, he refuses to accept the imperial badge which to him meant (wrongly, perhaps) desertion of the people, but trampled it under foot and in the act dies.

Sordello is psychological cousin-german to Pauline's lover, and his "story" as a narrative of events is upon a first reading unintelligible. Carlyle said there were only two lines in it he could understand, the first:

"Who will may hear Sordello's story told";
and the last,

"Who would has heard Sordello's story told."

Even a friendly hand is compelled to write: "It is one of the most incomprehensible in all literature." A minute knowledge of a most difficult piece of history —that of the Italian cities in the later Middle Ages—is presumed. But a scholarly reader would be perplexed by the confusion of fictitious with historical characters, and he would share the misery of an unlearned reader in being utterly unable to follow the thread of the story. The narrative goes backward and forward weaving a wellnigh inextricable web. Fortunately, a clue to Sordello has been furnished by a friendly hand in plain prose by which a patient reader may find his way.

When Browning set about Sordello he had learned that monologue—the recitation of an event by the author —was tiresome. Even given the specious appearance of dialogue, as in Paracelsus, the effect was the same. He somewhat changed the mode in Sordello, which is a monologue delivered in the third person. The qualities of the verse were the same, and the ideas to be brought out were the same as in Browning's previous work. "The historical decoration was purposely of no more importance than a background requires, and my stress lay on the incidents in the development of a soul." The only new factors in this story are mechanical ones.

In Paracelsus I called attention to a method by which Browning gave the closing scene in Paracelsus a good deal of life. The device was to have Paracelsus describe a dream. A description of an event by a third person has advantages; it can tell us about passive people, yet put action into the recital. If, on the contrary, inactive people were allowed to work out their own lives, or were set to describing their lives, which in performance, have been typical failures, no action could be expected. Had anyone else written Sordello I should call it a narrative poem. Since the poem in Browning's hands seems to be a new study in the development of monologue, I had rather think of it as a monologue in the third person.

The qualities that Browning wished to give the verse he succeeded in giving it. The poem has brilliancy and in parts action, in spite of the historical tangle which makes Sordello hard reading. For in movement Sordello resembles a man in pantomime, who, going through all the motions necessary for a vigorous progress, gains no ground and only signals the distance. The means by which he rescued his story from being wearisome, however, is not the most important discovery that Browning shows us in Sordello, for he uses monologue in the third person very rarely afterwards. The great discovery the

poet made, which must have rejoiced him as Cortez
rejoiced:

> "When with eagle eyes
> He stared at the Pacific . . ."

was Italy which he beheld from the Alpine heights of
his former flight. Browning's theological mind expressed
in monologue, had a tendency to syllogistic nakedness.
His lofty thought was as cold as the spaces are said to
be between the stars. In Italy he found not only a gor-
geous background for his ideas, but men and women
of rich natures to express his views of life. I cannot
conceive what he would have become as a literary
workman, had he not made the discovery to which I
call attention.

More metaphysical and more learned than any poet
of the century, many dangers lay in Browning's way.
A keener observer but with less fancy than Shelley, his
philosophy must have found another means of expression
from that displayed by his predecessor's bewildering
Muse. Without a disposition to repose in simple nature
like Wordsworth he could not have followed along the
path of the "Excursion." Unprofitable as it may be to
discuss such hypothetical questions, it was Italy, as far
as I can see, that saved to us Robert Browning, the
poet. Otherwise, his learning and his complex knowledge of the soul must have produced the most pedantic
and mystic verse imaginable. Such a catastrophe, for-

tunately, we have been spared, and in view of what the discovery of Italy was to Browning and to English poetry, an admirer is tempted to see a poetic justice in the fact that in Italy Mrs. Browning is buried, and that in Italy the poet himself breathed his last.

When once his Muse had found that sunny land, she rarely left it. The scenes of his greatest works are laid there, his masterpiece, "The Ring and the Book," "Lauria," "Pippa Passes" (his finest idyl or mask, to give it a name),—besides a host of lyrics and other pieces. Italy is the studio of Browning's art.

We have seen how Browning took up monologue, as Hamlet takes a bunch of rapiers, tested one or two forms, found imperfection in them, and rejected them. At last we saw him grasp the particular form best suited to his genius. In "The Ring and the Book," he found the broadest scope for his thought and a form adapted to his nature. Let us close our study of the development of his art with an examination of his masterpiece.

"The Ring and the Book" is a poem in blank verse and contains a little over twenty thousand lines, broken into twelve parts. In the first part, the plot is told by the poet, and also the incident that brought the story to his knowledge. A manuscript volume of law briefs, and letters picked up at a book-stall in Florence, is the "book" of the title. The "ring" is a poet's fancy. When an Etruscan jeweller wished to make a ring of the purest possible gold, he mixed the precious metal with an alloy.

The substance is then "a manageable mass." After he has formed and cut the ring to his wish, he removes with an acid the alloy,—

> "self sufficient now the shape remains,
> The rondure brave, the lilied loveliness,
> Gold as it was, is, shall be evermore,
> Prime nature with an added artistry—
> No carat lost, and you have gained a ring."

The poet compares himself to the goldsmith, and the fancy and "artistry" of the verse to the serviceable alloy which will evaporate when once the story, "pure gold," is fixed in the reader's mind. Each of the eleven remaining books, except the last, is given up to an actor in the events narrated, who rehearses the whole story from the side of his personal experience.

At Rome on Christmas night in 1697, a horrible murder was committed. "The Ring and the Book" is a history of the trial.

An old couple of some property, but of no social importance, give their daughter, Pompilia, a girl of thirteen, to Count Guido Franceschini. The Count, for his part, supplies a ruined fortune but an ancient name. He has spent his life in the household of a Cardinal, and at fifty discovers that he is still at the bottom of the ladder. The parents of Pompilia, Pietro and Violante, accompany their daughter to the estate of Guido in Arezzo, he being now master of their property. Life there is soon made intolerable for the old people, and they return to Rome. Once home they spread the report that Pompilia is not, after all, their daughter but a foundling from the dregs of the city. The story, though terrible, is true. Violante, to please her husband, and to secure the descent of some property, had pretended to give birth to a child that in fact she had received from a brothel. Pietro had been as much deceived as his neighbors.

A law-suit follows the disclosure, in which the old people try to recover Pompilia's dowry. The poor child, left to the mercy of the Count, has a miserable existence. When Guido comprehends her aversion to him, he becomes fiendishly vindictive and would willingly be rid of her, if he could still retain her dowry. After four years of torture, she can endure her position no longer, and to save her own soul, as well as the life of the child soon to be born, she flies to Rome with a young Canon, Giuseppe Caponsacchi. They are overtaken on the way by Guido, and are placed in custody. A trial of the case relegated the priest to an out-of-the-way village, sent Pompilia into the Convent for Penitents, and allowed the Count to return to Arezzo.

After a time Pompilia is permitted to dwell in the house of Pietro and Violante, who still love her, and there her son is born. On getting news of this, Guido takes four country lads, and plunges on to Rome, breaks in upon the family of his father-in-law and murders Pietro, Violante and Pompilia. The murderers flee blindly from the city, but are found in their bloody clothes asleep in a barn, where they had flung themselves overcome with fatigue. In spite of a multitude of wounds, Pompilia lives a few days, and tells the story of her life to a monk. The murderers are brought to trial; from the court the case is sent up to the Pope, for it was supposed that inasmuch as the Count belonged to one of the lower orders of priesthood, and came from a distinguished family, the papal decision would release the prisoners. This hope, however, was disappointed. The five murderers were put to death.

"A disgusting story" you will say "from beginning to end. There is foulness enough in poor Pompilia's nativity. You add to the pile Violante's fatal trick which gave her deceived husband a daughter. Next you heap up a mercenary marriage—an innocent child of thirteen forced into the arms of a brute of fifty. Then follows the flight of a wife with a priest; after that the murder of three people, and the execution of five more. Such a festering mass one would rather pass holding his nose. But no, you hail us to it and confide to us that it is a great poet's masterpiece of poetry." A critic inclined to such argument could go on at length against Browning's masterpiece. But when you examine the facts, you see that within their limits can be naturally discussed the questions that interest modern society. In these, for Browning, lay the value of the subject.

"The Ring and the Book" is a work of art of beautiful

design which holds not only wise thoughts about life and a great play of fancy, but a new creation to take place shall we say, among the immortals, Antigone, Desdemona, Ophelia, and their sisters.   We can imagine that Browning's great poem has this inscription—The name of the lady enshrined here is Pompilia.

Although Browning has given voice in his verse to so many men and women, few of them are our intimates. We smile, perhaps, as we think of Bishop Blougram with his worldly use of his office and his stout argumentative armour; he is real.   Fra Lippo Lippi is pretty distinct with the watchmen "fiddling" at his throat, and Pippa, too, with her song influencing so many lives as she passes along.

> "God's in his heaven
> All's right with the world."

Lucullus would approve of the few and select guests at the symposium of Browning's creations.   Perhaps the list could be enlarged.   Even a dinner-party after Byron's taste could be arranged "in number equal to the Muses," but no immortal like Hamlet or Lear among them, unless we ask Pompilia.   She is flesh and blood as Guido's hooked dagger proved.   Springing up out of the mud and resting upon dark waters, she is, always, "lilied loveliness."   She grew more like a flower than a human being.   No one taught her anything.   When her husband showed the court letters which he claimed she had written Caponsacchi, full of warm love, she defended herself by saying very simply that she knew neither how to read nor write.   She is not like the girls Roman art students paint—blank looking peasants with no soul in their faces.   Pompilia is a "woman-child" who on her death-bed could give right answers to most of the questions that make life perplexing.

"Marriage-making for the earth,
With gold so much,—birth, power, repute so much,
Or beauty, youth so much, in lack of these!
Be as the angels, rather, who apart
Know themselves into one, are found at length
Married but marry never, no, nor give
In marriage, they are man and wife at once
When the true time is: here we have to wait."

Hear her talking to Caponsacchi, the young Canon as they are whirled along in a carriage towards Rome.

"Tell me, are men unhappy in some kind
Of mere unhappiness at being men,
As women suffer being womanish?
　　　*　*　*　*　*　*　*　*
It hurts us if a baby hides its face
Or child strikes at us punily,—
　　　*　*　*　*　*　*　*　*
And strength may have its drawback weakness 'scapes."

A soul that meets nobly the experience of life will,

without schoolmasters or "the humanities," develop loveliness. Such is the poet's thesis in Pompilia.

"It was not given Pompilia to know much,
Speak much, to write a book, to move mankind,
Be memorized by who records my time.
Yet if in purity and patience, if
In faith held fast despite the plucking fiend
* * * If in right returned
For wrong, most pardon for worst injury,
If there be any virtue, and praise,—
Then will this woman-child have proved—who knows?—
Just the one prize vouchsafed unworthy me,
Seven years a gardener of the untoward ground
I till."

So speaks the Pope.

Caponsacchi, Pompilia's deliverer, stands before us
like another Theseus. We admire him and the progress
he made in understanding life through the sad part he
played. Yet in a way he is only a study of a young
Italian priest of the seventeenth century. He appreciates
Pompilia, that is his greatest recommendation. His
feeling for her is reverence like that for the holy Virgin
in the chancel of his cathedral.

"You know that this is not love, sirs, it is faith
The feeling that there's God, he reigns and rules
Out of this low world, that is all, no harm."

He is brave, he is pure, but as a poetic creature he lacks Pompilia's charm. He learned that God is served not only by administering the offices of the church, by writing verses for a pagan bishop, or by keeping his services to his fellows conventional. He discovered that he served God best when, after discovering Pompilia's plight, he had the courage to go to her rescue.

As for Count Guido, he is a thorough villain with so good an excuse for himself, if you please, that when he described his views of life to the court, the judges must have shifted uneasily in their chairs at the likeness of their own ideas to those of a murderer. For the rub was that Guido defended himself by syllogisms, the premises of which were everyday maxims in society. There was no doubt about the soundness of the premises, but the conclusions drawn from them unfortunately justified murder.

"Honor is a thing of value, for if I have it anyone connected with me is benefited." "Certainly," replied the world, "all hereditary nobility, all patrician power, is founded upon that fact." "Then if I share this valuable possession with someone who for value received gives me money, what is wrong about the transaction?" When Guido married Pompilia he has done that very thing. And the judges find it difficult to answer.

Roman law, it appears, would have upheld Guido in killing Pompilia had he done the deed after warm pursuit, when he confronted the runaways. Guido laug at such discrimination and in a step or two leads his judges to a point where logically they must admit his right to kill his wife when he did. "I may punish a disobedient servant, you say. When does the instrument cease to be allowable,—a switch, a stick, a pitchfork, a dagger, where should I have stopped?" Admit that the end justifies the means, then listen to Guido:—

> "I don't hear much of harm that Malchus did
> After the incident of the ear, my lords!
> Saint Peter took the efficacious way;
> Malchus was sore but silenced for his life:
> He did not hang himself i' the Potter's Field
> Like Judas, who was trusted with the bag
> And treated to sops after he proved a thief."

Guido is too much given to self-analysis to be a villain in real life, unless we call his sprightly psychology the Latin temperament. But when we have closed the book we find him shaping himself distinctly in our memories, and living by his own rights, a thorough rascal, like Iago.

Although the plot of The Ring and the Book is unique in poetry, we can see why Browning welcomed "the find." He wished from some central position to survey mankind and to dispense a large benevolence of observation. For this purpose he took a seat at the trial held in Rome. A trial in any court brings all sorts of odd intelligence to light; it ransacks past family history for generations; it is intolerant of privacy. A court is a rich laboratory for a philosopher who is a poet. From a seat by his friend the judge, he can look upon all conditions of life and can brood all social questions.

Browning secured these advantages by weaving his poem around a great trial. The bare facts of the case would retain their ugly look in a novel or in a play; prose would not sufficiently exalt them; the swift action of drama would not afford them covering. Yet a plot like this, ranging from a harlot to a pope, is necessary if Browning is to give full scope to his powers.

The four rustics who had a hand in the murder offer a study in primitive human nature. They were not vicious, merely ruddy human animals. "A goat to kill or a man, what is the difference?" is their pose. "Such," says Browning, "was man in a state of nature; such were the vaunted denizens of the Golden Age." From their brutishness to Pompilia's spirituality is, indeed, a range. Hence the choice of the plot.

How interesting, too, to hand a bundle of cases, in ethics and theology to the final earthly appeal, for those days, in such matters. The pope who figures as the final judge of the questions is painted in the white and gold of Fra Angelico's monastery walls.

The form of the poem within its limits is as rigid as that of the lyric, epic or the drama. It is not merely eight or ten different ways of telling the same story. The construction is carefully planned; the mould is unique. A monologue, when talked into the air, like the "Mad-house Cells" could be censured on the ground that it was unnatural. People, it is true, do mutter, do soliloquize, and doubtless so superior a company as Browning's *dramatis personae* might offer the same excuse as the man in the anecdote, taxed with talking to himself. "I suppose I fell into the habit from liking to converse with a sensible person." Andrea del Sarto is a good subject for monologue, as he vainly explores for doors to Lucrezia's mind; so is Fra Lippo Lippi over-persuading the watchmen who have caught him in a frolic.

Even a monologue addressed to someone named in the poem becomes unnatural when it takes on the length of Bishop Blougram's apology. That worthy ecclesiastic, notwithstanding his good table, would hardly get many men to sit through more than one such harangue. In fact, the Bishop's table-companion in the present case, once released, flies to the uttermost parts of the earth. A man either could not talk so uninterruptedly, or he would not be permitted to.

In "The Ring and the Book" many of the features we object to in the earlier monologues have disappeared. Pompilia's confession to the Augustinian is a natural monologue; so is a lawyer's plea, the statement of a witness (if he is bold and fortunate); a story that one has to tell; a letter and a sermon—all are natural monologues. These are what the separate parts of the poem contain, except the introduction in part one, and the section called The Pope. Each person tells his story without interruption—Pompilia to the monk, Guido and Caponsacchi to the judges, the lawyers rehearse their speeches.

There is something else in "The Ring and the Book" that reminds one of Greek dramas. The three great choruses, Half Rome, the Other Half Rome, and Tertium Quid, although confined to their sections in the first part of the poem, ring out the changes of the popular mind like Strophe, Antistrophe and Epode.

Apart from the general arrangements, there is a studied effect produced by the choice of characters, and the particular sections of the poem they command. The lawyer, Hyacinthus de Archangelis, is the comedian of the piece, and like Shakespeare's fools, he relieves for a little our depression, and creates an appetite again for serious parts. His brother-lawyer we might call the satirist of the poem. Johannes-Babtiste Bottenus is not satirical in his words, nor is Hyacinthus consciously a humorist, but after the reader has been carried away by Pompilia's woes, he is suddenly brought face to face with the selfishness of Johannes and the good-nature of Hyacinthus, the effect is equal to keen satire and broad comedy. These lawyers look at the whole subject, suffering, sin, murder, trial, and all, as something sent in the providence of God to help their fame a little, or to give their children an extra allowance of bread and butter.

We have come to the end of our review of Browning's use of monologue. If there were time it would be interesting to examine his art in the details of technique.

The bold, vivid portraits he dashes off in a line or two should claim our attention; his frequent use of alliteration and the other amenities of style which he is thought to care little about; the wonderful imagery by which he helps us understand the subtle moods of the soul. In his early poems, similes stood out from the body of the verse, as a button painted by Meissonier would stand out on the blouse of one of Millet's peasants. In the later poems the tone of the whole has been raised to the brilliancy of the early figures. But these minute studies hardly concern us here, engaged as we have been upon the monologue as a whole.

The art of Browning in monologue was developed, it would seem, as a consequence of moral qualities in himself and his time, and of an evolutionary moment exhibited in English verse. He shared the seriousness of his generation and wished to teach it the meaning of body and soul. He chose a poetic form, monologue, because that form permitted a combination of action and description, where his personal interpretation of the story might at any time intrude. This method led naturally to a cold, metaphysical and lifeless treatment of his subjects, which were little more than abstractions, until the discovery of Italy as a rich storehouse of traditions, personages and incidents fortunately rescued him, and gave his themes warmth and motion. Browning is never truly a dramatic poet,—one who lets life act itself freely before his readers. He muses upon life, to be sure, in vigorous speech but still in terms of the intellect rather than in terms of action. He is analytical, searching the consciousness of his characters for motives, moods and spiritual processes, and these he expounds with all the virile brilliancy of his strong nature and with all the egoism associated with soliloquy.

Browning at his best made the appeal of a deeper confession of experience, in a direct and conversational style; he uncovered the realities behind English conventionalities.

In his "My Last Dutchess," "Any Wife to Any Husband," "The Statue and the Bust," Browning notified his readers that they might think and talk straight about problems essential to their lives. He gave courage to the expression of natural emotion. Byron and Shelley led foreign revolts. Browning a domestic reformation.

Browning had a theological method but he indulged in a sincerity of expression about sex that gave a sense of support and liberation to many minds that puritanism had confused, and that the new paganism had alarmed.

Browning gave English and American women a new sense of social and religious freedom without the loss of their comfort and respectability. Byron was too foreign and too robust. In Browning there is homeopathic liberty with allopathic conservatism of behavior. The lover and husband of Elizabeth Barrett could be followed even when he seemed ranging on dangerous moral grounds.

His marriage was incalculably ideal according to English notions—romantic and conventional. The result was literary acceptance even when not understood. In fact, perhaps his challenge of style obscured what otherwise might have been a challenge of subject matter. For no poet of his generation except Swinburne talked so plainly about fleshly things.

But Browning's language was stronger than his thought. He never went far in social emancipation and he did not go so far as his wife went in political emancipation. Even the young Canon in "The Ring and the Book" is held in; this Renaissance Sir Galahad was only fitted out with a sense of duty, and was allowed no heart flutterings in his rescue of the Countess.

After all, Browning, the poet, lived in an English park in which one section was a wild garden. He strolled about from one part of the park to another, dressed in the habiliments of an Alpine climber and, on occasions, he sat down for long periods on a bench.

The Religion of Shakespeare

WHEN we assemble in a cathedral to celebrate the 350th anniversary of Shakespeare's birth, and the celebration in which we participate is one of thousands of gatherings, official and informal, for a like purpose, we involuntarily ask ourselves an unpleasant question: What if Shakespeare were not, after all, the author of the works that bear his name? What if Francis Bacon wrote the plays we have witnessed when we went to the theatre to "see Shakespeare." For us to honor a man with fervid enthusiasm for work, achieved by another, would make us ridiculous.

The question, "Did Bacon write Shakespeare?" admits fortunately of a brief, satisfactory answer; one that can quickly relieve our minds without plunging us into the recondite reckonings of modern cabalists.

Bacon did not possess a powerful imagination. For this reason he was not a great man of science, for imagination is essential to scientific discovery.* If Francis Bacon had too little imagination to be a great scientist, he certainly had too little imagination to be a great poet. He surely could not have produced the greatest creatures of the imagination in modern literature.

*Karl Pearson's Grammar of Science, p 34, note.

[75]

Shakespeare overtopped other dramatists by the power of his imagination. He did not excel in technique; nor in plot; but in characterization and poetry. That is to say, he excelled in spiritual construction and beauty by sheer force of imagination. The imaginative quality of Shakespeare's work will be that which appeals more and more to his admirers.

But why concern ourselves about the religion of Shakespeare? "The play is the thing." Why query about the creed of the playwright? Besides, the drama being an objective picture of life, what would be the criterion for deciding which of the views expressed by his characters were his own, and which were selected merely as suitable to his *dramatis personnae?*

Fortunately for us, outside the list of Shakespeare's plays there are poems amd sonnets which strike so personal a note that we cannot help but believe they express the poet's own opinion. Those we can study for information about Shakespeare's religion. Well, then, suppose Shakespeare did leave a confession of faith, how does that concern us who have the plays?

A man's religious views sum up what he considers to be the underlying principles of his life as well as his motives for action. To gain an idea of what the greatest English poet conceived to be fundamental to our deepest experiences, as motive, as purpose, as reward, would not only paint the poet's portrait spiritually, but would seem to relate him in a substantial fashion to humanity —which loves intimate portraiture.

By religion, most of us mean belief in creeds, dogmas, rites, sacraments, holy hopes. In searching out Shakespeare's religion we should probably ask, Did Shakespeare believe in God? Did he believe in the life of the soul after death? Did he believe in prayer? Does he show interest in the general Christian way of describing religious experiences as a theological scheme of incarnation, atonement, et cetera? What does he say about the soul, sin, justice, truth?

We shall be disappointed in Shakespeare's religion if we study it from this ordinary standpoint. But, at any rate, we shall be upon familiar ground; we shall be employing customary standards.

A surmise of the poet's religion might be hazarded from the attitude of great minds in the Elizabethan age. The notable event of the 16th Century was its break with religious authority (brought about by the Protestant Reformation) and its turning from scholasticism to nature.

So it is a significant fact that one of our few Shakespeare autographs is found in a copy of Montaigne's Essays—Montaigne, the skeptic. Emancipated from the scholastic tyrannies of mediaeval thought, Montaigne's freedom in the treating of life as he saw it, has given him a permanent place in literature.

Montaigne was thirty-one years old when Shakespeare

was born. The Essays were published when Shakespeare was a boy of sixteen. If they fell into his hands during the 1580's, they must have powerfully affected his youth. Montaigne's father was by birth an Englishman. The great essayist himself found inspiration in the Roman philosophy of Seneca and Plutarch. He adjusted the New Protestantism to the Old Catholicism by a tolerance which sprang from his individualism and from his doubt of absolute truth.

England was a land of Protestants and of Catholics held together by the elastic offices of the Book of Common Prayer. Montaigne solved some of Shakespeare's problems and showed in himself the sort of man religiously that Shakespeare depicted in his heroes, his kings and courtiers. The type of man the dramatist most sympathetically dealt with outside of the historical plays did not parade religion, but was polite, philosophical, tolerant to religious usages and to the mysteries in human life upon which formal religion is built up.

This skeptical attitude is characteristic of those who are bound for any reason to old institutions and yet feel the call of new ideas. Such minds are arranged in compartments. In some of those compartments action is loyal to tradition by force of habit or by reason of advantage; while in others action eagerly follows free and independent thought.

We find in the plays a respectful treatment of the church and its officials, not only the English Church

[78]

but the Church of Rome. We find also great use made
of the supernatural not merely for the purposes of the
theatre, but as though it constituted in the author's
thought the veritable background of life. Macbeth,
Hamlet, The Tempest, are almost based upon the
supernatural. Hamlet's remark:
"There are more things in heaven and earth, Horatio,
  Than are dreamed of in your philosophy"
has so sincere a ring as to incline one to feel that the
thought could not have been indifferent to Shakespeare
himself. But while Shakespeare was superstitious
toward the invisible world, and religiously complaisant
toward this world, he too, like Montaigne, studied life
with a free mind.

Skepticism—a formal holding to the old and waving
an enthusiastic greeting to the new—is the religious
attitude of intellectual leaders in the ancient and modern
world, whose particular distinction has been that while
they felt the present to be founded upon the past, they
themselves were inspirers of the future. Socrates bade
Crito to offer a cock to Aesculepius at the moment he
was to suffer death for his atheism. Matthew Arnold
denied the fundamental dogmas of Christianity yet
united with his fellows in divine worship in Christian
churches.

If we look into Shakespeare's sonnets and poems for
specific religious utterances, we may, I said, be disappointed. We do not find, for instance, such use of the

[79]

word God as to convince us that Shakespeare held to a belief in a personal deity.

This silence or non-commitment is the more remarkable because in his time many men of high poetic power wrote on distinctly religious themes. Sir Philip Sidney translated the Psalms. Donne wrote divine poems. One was called The Soul's Progress. Constable wrote sacred sonnets. The master of all writers of sonnets, Petrarch, two centuries earlier used Biblical phrases. (Compare Sonnet 15). But in Shakespeare I cannot find any of these evidences of conventional religious interest—certainly not a use of religious phraseology.

Shakespeare did not deal with the love of God but the love of men and women. He knew love as it played a part in human life. He did not speculate. He did not feign satisfaction for the deep longings of his own heart, as Dante had done, by devising pictures of immortal lovers. When he felt despair at the thought of love's brief life, circumscribed by human existence, he could only guess that love might survive the grave; might conquer death—the longer by reason of the finer material of the memorial—namely, his poetry. He made memory the only immortality.

> "Not mine own fears, nor the prophetic soul
> Of the wide world, dreaming on things to come,
> Can yet the lease of my true love control,
> Suppos'd as forfeit to a confin'd doom.

The mortal moon hath her eclipse endur'd,
And the sad augurs mock their own presage;
And peace proclaims olives of endless age.
Now with the drops of this most balmy time
My love looks fresh, and Death to me subscribed
Since, spite of him, I'll live in this poor rhyme,
While he insults o'er dull and speechless tribes:
And thou in this shall find thy monument,
When tyrants' crests and tombs of brass are spent."

Sonnet 107.

But what did our poet consider death to be? This is a pertinent question for the student of Shakespeare's religion, since religion in the past has been so largely concerned with the fate of the dead and with the unseen world. The tone of the sonnets is not hopeful. Inferences drawn from chance lines rather than from deliberate treatment may not be considered the strongest arguments; yet what is positive in a man gets said. Blanco White's line:

"If light can thus deceive, wherefore not life,"

and Milton's line:

"They also serve who only stand and wait"

fix the hopes and beliefs of the authors as well as a volume. But among the two thousand lines in the sonnets, there is no such hopeful utterance about death. "Death's dateless night"; "the edge of doom"; "That fell arrest without all bail"; "churl death," these are the sonnet's description of death.   Shakespeare sees no light through death's door.   His doubt, his wish against his doubt, and his hopelessness in sonnets 71, 73, and 74 are painful.

He bids his friend:

"No longer mourn for me when I am dead
  Than you shall hear the surly, sullen bell
  Give warning to the world that I am fled
  From this vile world, with vilest worms to dwell."

                                                    Sonnet 71.

But this thought is too terrible and he hastens to exhort the friend to love him well for there are but a few more years left for friendship.   Then he comforts himself with a poor pretense.   His verse, he says, contains his true self and spirit, which will survive his death and will remain with his friend.

Death is so terrible a destroyer that the only way to meet it is to have shorn one's self during one's life of all it can take away.   This is asceticism without the anchorite's hope of future rewards.

"Poor soul, the centre of my sinful earth,
  Fooled by those rebel powers that thee array,
  Why dost thou pine within and suffer dearth,
  Painting thy outward walls so costly gay?
  Why so large cost, having so short a lease,
  Dost thou upon thy fading mansion spend?

Shall worms, inheritors of this excess,
Eat up thy charge? Is this thy body's end?
Then, soul, live thou upon thy servant's loss,
And let that pine to aggravate thy store;
Buy terms divine in selling hours of dross;
Within be fed, without be rich no more;
So shalt thou feed on Death, that feeds on men,
And Death once dead, there's no more dying then."

Sonnet 146.

On the other hand, Shakespeare's sense of sin as of a wrong done to the soul of man, is keen.

"The expense of spirit in a waste of shame
   Is lust in action; and till action, lust
   Is perjur'd, murd'rous, bloody, full of blame."

Sonnet 129.

Shakespeare hates sin as much as any Puritan but regards it not as a rebellion against God but a wrong done by the body against the soul, to be loathed because it wastes man's spirit. Yet sin, he thinks, has its ordered place in the scheme of the world; it is not an unexpected intruder or ultimately antagonistic to the good.

"O benefit of ill! now I find true
   That better is by evil still made better."

Sonnet 119.

Shakespeare, as Josiah Royce remarks, came to a stronger faith through evil experiences and made a better

[83]

success of his life than did Milton, who was the greater idealist.

Although the Christian religion is built around the idea of the sinfulness of man, and Shakespeare detested sin, I cannot find any signs in the sonnets of his sympathy with Christianity. The absence of avowed opinion is not, of course, conclusive.

But Christianity is an aggressive faith. Concealment of the faith has been among Christians a reproach. Love poems may not be the best instruments for the expression of religious belief, yet Spenser found beauty in biblical imagery and thus addressed his mistress:

"Thou glorious image of the maker's beautie
My soverayne saynt, the Idoll of my thought
 *   *   *   *   *   *   *
And of the brood of angels heavenly born
And with the crew of blessed saints unborn."

Amoretti Sonnet 61.

Spenser not only referred to God but called him maker. The word God (spelled with a capital), I do not remember once in Shakespeare's sonnets, even as an exclamation. The words heaven and hell are used, but how? In Sonnet 29 we find the line:

"And trouble deaf heaven with my bootless cries."

This is the voice of neither a pagan or a Christian. It sounds very much like the cry of modern materialism.

Again, in the following lines, we have the word heaven used perhaps in the conventional way, but the limiting word "my" quickly turns it into a metaphorical meaning.

"Then give me welcome, next my heaven the best,
Even to thy pure and most most loving breast."
Sonnet 110.

Usually Shakespeare uses the words heaven and hell figuratively, as to "pass a hell of time"; again, speaking of pleasures that bear a very bitter fruit, he says:

"Yet none knows well
To shun the heaven that leads men to this hell."
Sonnet 129.

Sonnet 121 has sometimes been interpreted as a rebuke to the Puritans and their contempt for the theatre. It begins with the quatrain:

" 'Tis better to be vile than vile esteemed,
When not to be receives reproach of being;
And the just pleasure lost, which is so deemed,
Not by our feeling, but by others' seeing."
Sonnet 121.

At any rate, it is a protest against a theory we hear advanced even now that conduct should not only be stainless but that it should be devoid of offense.

Another slap at the Puritan theology was contained in Sonnet 105, "Let not my love be called idolatry." The best human emotions must not be given bad names.

When Shakespeare threw his glance upon life as a whole, what did he think of it as indicated in his sonnets? He is saddened by the similarity of man's position in the world to that of all other material things (Son. 15). He sees everywhere "simple truth miscall'd simplicity," and "captive good attending captain ill." (Son. 66.) He thinks the world has deteriorated from a time.

> "When beauty liv'd and died as flowers do now,
>   Before these bastard signs of fair were born,
>   Or durst inhabit on a living brow;
>   Before the golden tresses of the dead,
>   The right of sepulchres, were shorn away,
>   To live a second life on second head."
>
> Sonnet 68.

The more I read the sonnets, the more I feel the sadness of their tone. Not a wail, not an imaginary burden like that of some 19th Century poets, but a terrible suppressed apprehension that the doom of man may be a death that has no waking. The feeling sometimes thrown off, repeatedly returns. Then he draws closer to his friend; then he is sure that love is the only divine thing, and the beauty, truth and constancy in our lives the jewels to be cherished.

Shakespeare's religion is not of the conventional kind—it is not essentially supernatural nor is it dogmatic; it also utterly fails to disclose belief in the usual tenets and symbols of Christianity. Shakespeare's religion is the worship of the power of love. Shakespeare understood from personal experience the transforming power that love possesses as witnessed by St. John, and he has written almost identical words,

St. John:
> "And all mine are thine, and thine are
> mine; and I am glorified in them."

Shakespeare in "Let the bird of loudest lay,"
> "So they loved, as love in twain
> Had the essence but in one."

Professor George Herbert Palmer, of Harvard University, discovers in Shakespeare's sonnets a progressive and deeply spiritual experience. Many of his sonnets call upon the young man, to whom the first 126 were written, not to permit his beauty and graces to perish from the earth, but to perpetuate them. Beyond this conception of a "natural immortality," Shakespeare proceeds to a view of "ideal immortality," to be secured his friend by the praises of undying verse. From this ideal immortality he advances to an "intellectual and spiritual immortality," "in which we know ourselves as moral beings, capable of commanding circumstances instead of accepting their compulsions."

"Here is Spiritual Immortality. Man is a spirit, no mere creature of circumstance, passive, instantaneous, dependent on alien forces within and without, which sweep him along their blind current, regardless of any good of his own. He is an active being, dictatorial over time and circumstances, with power to compel chance and change to work for his permanent welfare. Such an understanding of immortality, grounded in the nature of personality, gives a hope more specific than the Ideal Immortality of fame, more humanly significant than the Natural Immortality of 'breed'."

That this immortality which so exalts personality and its control of the outward can control death, would seem to be a by-product of Prof. Palmer's idea of personality as participating in the Absolute. Outside of Hegelianism, such a leaping across the chasm of death may not be easy to reason—only to faith.

Shakespeare, as the poet of feudalism, upholds the aristocracy and laughs at the people in a way that will probably provoke in the future more criticism and secure for his work less popular attention than in the past. At any rate, his is not a religion which derives its significance from service—it is not a religion of humanity.

Shakespearian official religion would seem to be a superstition of supernaturalism, with a polished tolerance for existing and established forms, but only sincere and vital in so far as it was a belief in the laws of spiritual growth, through high relationship, love and loyalty.

[88]

Shakespearian personal religion is not the religion of humanity; nor is it dogmatic faith, nor is it a mysticism; but the perception of the creative and transforming power of love and the destructive spiritual power of all that contradicts this highest union.

Shakespeare is so large a part of English Literature and of current dramatic attention that we never think of him as belonging to the Middle Ages. Yet if he is to be placed religiously, it must be with the thought of the Middle Ages, or at best with the transition period between the Middle Ages and modern times. The characteristic of the transition was the extreme one-sidedness of the religious attitude—mysticism concentrated on God, skepticism concentrated upon the world.

In Shakespeare's religion we see the beginning of a new harmony—the harmony of modern life—a world constructed by spiritual causes. We also see tne method: viz., an individual spiritual experience which proceeds to interpret life and to mould life freely according to its own experiences.

Shakespeare learned subjectively, yet by means of a relationship, the spiritual laws of the soul: First, the creative power of love:

"Love is too young to know what conscience is;
Yet who knows not, conscience is born of love."
—Sonnet 151.

[89]

Secondly, the unifying power of love:

> "Two distinct, division none,*
> Number there in love was slain."

Thirdly, the denial of ownership:

> "Either was the other's mine."
> Property was thus appalled
> That the self was not the same
> Single nature's double name
> Neither two nor one was called."

Fourthly, the deeper rationality of love:

> "Love hath reason, reason none
> If what parts can so remain."

All this sounds very much like St. John's Gospel. Both have a modern side.

The new idea of the individual and of society cannot better be fulfilled than by the religious exaltation of Jesus:

> "All mine are thine and thine are mine."

But this was also the spiritual experience of Shakespeare.

When we have the power to transform life, proceeding from out of life itself; a capacity to destroy selfish isolation and to secure social identification and service, how far can the spiritual construction of life be carried? We

---

*Threnody in "The Passionate Pilgrim."

do not know. We believe it can substitute freedom for authority; peace for war; co-operation for hatred and antagonism; respect in place of arrogance; worship for lust; and service for exploitation.

Can spiritual construction of life also create immortality? Is it in itself everlasting? Is it a power eternal? We do not know. Only an act of faith permitted by the marvels of the soul's power and accomplishment in this life can give us hope and comfort and belief in the life to come.

Feodor Dostoevsky

TURGENEV called Dostoevsky mad. His disposition was morbid, his experiences tragic, his theories fantastic. If his friend Turgenev, of the same race, generation and art understood him so little as to question his sanity, how can one of a different race, era and profession set him before you clothed and in his right mind; some one to be warmly concerned with?

A clergyman is breathing his native air in Dostoevsky's world. Superstition, instinct, spiritual refinements of experience and tortures of soul, confessions, forgiveness, faith, the supernatual, the wisdom of babes, the inspiration of the humble and hurt, renunciation, sacred scriptures, national churches, inexorable divine law, transitoriness, weakness, simplicity, meekness, sinfulness, pity, patience, gentle judgment, despair, perdition—these emanations of humanity have already for the clergyman a personality. They are his familiars. When the clergy discover Dostoevsky they will go crazy over him as in the last century they did over Wordsworth, Browning and Tolstoi. He is an individualist, so are they; he believes all the forces of life are from within, so do they; he believes in the child-spirit as voicing the deity, so do they; he believes in the miracles, in immortality, in the Bible as do they. He obeyed dreams and presentiments. But I am going too far. While I am underpinning my own authority as a writer about Dostoevsky, I fear that I am weakening the authority of Dostoevsky himself.

Yes, he is a preacher, but cannot be confined in any group. That is what astonishes me. This Russian novelist of narrow intensities, of national prejudices, of old-fashioned limitations, not up-to-the-times, and lacking international sympathies, hating Germany, ill at ease in Italy, is a nut that must be cracked before we can enjoy our modernity, our internationalism, our improved conditions, our democratic equalities, our science.

I have found out several unexpected things about Dostoevsky:

(1) He has had a more extraordinary personal history than any of the writers of our times.

(2) He is a propagandist of Christian mysticism beyond any modern in literature.

(3) He is the voice of old Russia in its racial and instinctive inspirations as against the incoming of western ideas—modern science, Roman Catholicism, Socialism, western Europe's belief in force, etc.

(4) He actually has a place in the philosophy of the 19th Century as being the writer whose gospel of struggle through weakness, excited Nietzsche to such antagonism as to produce his gospel of the "will to power" and "the superman."

(5) He is a profound psychologist. He mined deeper into his characters than any modern writer. He discovered the new psychology before the psychiatrists. The region he displayed has become the Golconda of modern philosophy.

II.

DOSTOEVSKY'S father was a doctor (connected with a hospital for the poor of Moscow); his mother was the daughter of a Moscow merchant. Although his family was of noble origin, it no longer belonged to the large or small landowning class of assured income (as did Turgenev and Tolstoi) but to the lower and undistinguished professional class of precarious incomes. The need of money was almost as much at the front door of Dostoevsky's life, as it was of Balzac's. His lack of means has to be remembered at every step of his literary work: in his feverish choice of subject; in his desperate rush to complete his task; in his prolixities of treatment, which gave him in magazine form a larger price for his product; and in the worries that clouded his most productive days.

As a young man, after initial literary success, which placed him at the age of twenty-three among the literary leaders of his country, he became a student of French Socialism, of the mild, Fourier, co-operative type. He was arrested along with a group of similar-minded friends and was condemned to death. While waiting in a public square for the execution of the sentence (all the youths were to be shot), a reprieve came and a commutation of the sentence from death to exile in Siberia. A young man of applauded literary gifts, the rival of Turgenev, who was two years his senior, he was turned out of Europe into Asia; out of the society of intellectuals into that of criminals; out of civilization into frontier existence; and, worst of all, he was denied the use of his gifts.

Dostoevsky came back from Siberia a conservative; a great criminal psychologist; a genius without the right to publish his writing; a suppliant for the expression of his pent up thought. He also brought back from Siberia almost an old man's confidence in the national institutions and instincts of the Russian nation. Dostoevsky surrendered and abjured quite sincerely his Socialist philanderings. He bowed in quiet submission to the Autocrat of all the Russias without *arrière pensée*. He worshipped the national consciousness. He plunged backward and downward into the depths of Russian experiences and forsook the path of European economic and social ideas.

The bare chronology of his life is significant:

1821. Born in Moscow
1837. Entered Military School of Engineers
1843. Left Military School with rank of sub-lieutenant
1844. Left the Army
1846. Published "Poor Folk"
1849. Arrested (April 23)

1849. Reprieved from the scaffold and sentenced to Siberia (December 22)

1854. Became a common soldier

1856. Made a non-commissioned officer

" Regained the rank of officer

1857. Married Madame Issaev

1858. Right of hereditary nobility restored. Left the Army

1860. Returned to St. Petersburg

1861. Published "Injury and Insult"

" Published "Buried Alive"

1862. Visited the continent of Western Europe for the first time

1864. Death of his wife and of his brother Michael

1866. Published "Crime and Punishment"

1867. Married Anna Grigorievna Snitkin

" Published "The Gambler"

1868. Published "The Idiot"

1871. Published "The Possessed"

" Returned to St. Petersburg

1876. Commenced "The Diary of a Writer"

1879-80. Finished "The Brothers Karamazov"

1881. Died in St. Petersburg

The list of his works is quickly counted.

"Poor Folk"

"The Double"

"Mr. Prokharchin"

"The Landlady"

[96]

"A Weak Heart"
"Stepanchikovo Village"
"Sleepless Nights"
"The Honest Thief"
"The Friend of the Family"
"Uncle's Dream"
"Injury and Insult"
"Buried Alive"
"Crime and Punishment"
"The Gambler"
"The Idiot"
"The Permanent Husband"
"The Possessed"
"The Hobbledehoy"
"The Underground Spirit"
"The Diary of a Writer"
"The Brothers Karamazov"

Modern Russian art did not have as a foundation the ideals, the methods, or the masterpieces that western Europe inherited from the Middle Ages. The 13th Century, so boasted about in the west, was an epoch in Russia of Mongol invasion; the beginning of centuries of barbarous warfare. Not until the middle of the 18th Century was the Russian language fitted for literary use by Lomonosov. The University of Moscow was then founded and the Imperial Academy of Arts.

The Russia that we know was born of the French Revolution and the invasion of Napoleon. Yet her

reaction was almost Oriental. Her land lapsed back
into inactivity.

"She heard his legions thunder by,
Then plunged in dreams again."

Her writers (a brood born with the waning Napoleon)
offered largely a religious cure for the hurts of the
Russian soul. While Germany was perfecting a system
of education and working toward political unity; while
France after reaction was developing subsequent revolution, and carrying out the ideas of '92; while England
after reaction was battling in her Parliament for political
and economic reforms, Russia was reaching a profounder
self-consciousness, not through industrial, political or
educational institutions (Russia was denied these agen-
cies) but through poetry, fiction, painting and music—
this to the point of imminent revolution; for revolutions
are moments of supreme insight. As time went on,
Russia developed reforms, but they proceeded from
influence brought to bear upon the autocrat of Russia;
they were not the outgrowth of an orderly political evolution. Like wounds that heal dangerously from the top,
they had to be cut open afresh for deeper healing.

Russia, then, which had no Middle Ages or Renaissance; no early bloom corresponding to the *cinque-cento*
burst forth in the post-Napoleonic decade with a storage
of energy, a treasury of national legend, traits, customs,

folk song, ballad, and a range of influence that carried her art into the front rank. Russia produced giants.

Among the towering personalities, who created Russian art (Pushkin, Glinka, Gogol, Turgenev and Tolstoi) was Dostoevsky. Profoundly influenced by Dickens, Balzac, Victor Hugo and by the Russian Dickens, Gogol, he is nevertheless different from his literary masters. He is an entirely new literary product, as appears not only in the depth of his human studies, but in the intense nationalism of his point of view, as well as in his antagonism to European ideas. When I read Dostoevsky's eloquent diatribes against western science, I am reminded of the arguments launched against our own American civilization by visiting Hindus, Buddhists, Theosophists, Bahaists. They exalt the passivity of the Orient, which they misname spirituality; they decry the bigness, force and rush of the west, which they label materialism.

In personal appearance Dostoevsky gives one the impression of racial characteristics that, while peculiarly Russian, are neither patrician nor peasant.

Dostoevsky had light red hair; a thin beard; blue eyes; a somewhat narrow intensity of vision, with sweetness of expression and an appearance of cultivation. He had not the beauty of Turgenev—that Russian type that compares in appearance to Americans like Longfellow, nor had he the mujik-like features of Tolstoi.

In temperament he was highly neurotic. When a young man he developed epilepsy. He was also pestered by what psychologists call the delusion of reference—a nervous egoism so sensitive that everything which happens, or which others do and say, is regarded as having sinister personal reference.

The story of his break with Turgenev illustrated his temperamental ill-health. Having been invited by Turgenev to a party in St. Petersburg (just fancy, they were both distinguished, the host of 25 and the guest of 23). Dostoevsky turned up late. As he entered the room he heard the assemblage's laughter. He imagined that they were laughing at him and beat a hasty retreat; rushed out-of-doors without a hat and paced the sidewalk for an hour or two. Worse still, on account of this absurd fancy he bore a grudge for years against Turgenev. Is it to be wondered at that Turgenev called him mad?

Dostoevsky's nature was not sociable or attuned to polite, conventional intercourse. He was egotistic, gloomy, dictatorial—very sensitive in his friendships with men and women. He was easily offended and made much of misunderstandings. He was unlike Turgenev, the man of the world; or Tolstoi, the man of the fields. He was the man of a single city—St. Petersburg—where he led a submerged and gloomy life. "I live! I am in a thousand torments, but I live! I am on the pillory, but I exist! I see the sun, or I did not see the sun, but I know that it is there. And to know that there is a sun is enough."

An indefatigable worker, he did not allow his epileptic fits, which shattered his strength, to keep him from his desk but a day or two. "Believe me, dear (he wrote his niece) I literally toil day and night; if I am not precisely writing, I am walking up and down the room smoking and thinking of my work."* To his friend, Maikov, he writes from Vevey: "I intend in any event to go back to Russia. To get the book done, I must sit at my desk for at least eight hours daily.

"I have grown quite stupid from sheer hard work, and my head feels as if it were in pieces."†

He had dramatic talent, like his English admiration, Dickens. He was a masterly reader and declaimer of poetry and gave public recitations from the Russian.

His chirography was nice. His letters were carefully formed and compared in beauty to the manuscript of Dumas père.

He had the faults of pride, of haste, and of misinterpretations, but he did not have the faults of selfishness or meanness. His character was singularly rich in the Christian virtues, which he lauded—gentleness, a deep patience (in spite of hasty action), conscientious work, self-sacrifice for others. His inner life was patterned on Bible teachings; for to him the Bible was the greatest of books.

To his friend, N. L. Osmidov, he wrote: "I recommend you to read the whole Bible through in the Russian translation. The book makes a remarkable impression

*Letters, p. 153. †Letters, p. 149.

when one thus reads it. One gains, for one thing, the conviction that humanity possesses, and can possess, no other book of equal significance."*

In another letter he bids his friend "think of the noblest words that ever yet were spoken: I desire love and not sacrifice."†

Baron Vrangel, who was with him in Siberia and knew him all his life, said: "Dostoevsky's indulgence for everyone was quite extraordinary. He found excuses for even the worst of human traits and explained them all by defective education, the influence of environment, and inherited temperament." "Ah, my dear Alexander Yegorovitch, God has made men so, once for all!" he used to say. He sympathized with all who were abandoned by destiny, with all the unhappy, ill and poor. Everyone who knew him well knows of his extraordinary goodness of heart.

In Dostoevsky the great Russian traits of pity and patience were illustrated. From Siberia he wrote: "I'll rejoice greatly that I find there is patience in my soul for quite a long time yet, that I desire no earthly possessions and need nothing but books, the possibility of writing and of being daily for a few hours alone."‡ He shows an unworldliness suitable to his own monks who are such high personages spiritually, and so likeable.

He hated Europe; but in order to escape imprisonment for debt in St. Petersburg, he had to live out of his sacred

*Letters, p. 233. †Letters, p. 297. ‡Letters, p. 71.

Russia for several years. Dostoevsky had, too, the discipline of sorrow. Death sentence, exile, imprisonment, poverty and a second exile for debt, then bereavement following bereavement, were all crowded into his three score years. Loss brought him not only sorrow but domestic responsibility. After the death of his wife and daughter, when his brother died, he took upon himself the support of his brother's family.

Listen to a simple, sorrowing heart: "My Sonia is dead; we buried her three days ago. Two hours before her death I did not know that she was to die. The doctor told us, three hours before she died, that things were going better and she would live. She was only a week ill; she died of inflammation of the lungs."

"Ah, my dear Apollon Nikolayevitch, my love for my first child was probably most comical; I dare say I expressed it most comically in my letters to all who congratulated me. I have doubtless been ridiculous in everybody's eyes, but to you, to YOU, I am not ashamed to say anything. The poor little darling creature, scarcely three months' old, had already, for me, individuality and character. She was just beginning to know and love me, and always smiled when I came near. And now they tell me, to console me, that I shall surely have other children. But where is Sonia? Where is the little creature for whom I would, believe me, gladly have suffered death upon the cross, if she could have remained alive?"*

*Letters, p. 147.

III

No country of Europe seems to reflect so immediately in its emotional life the phases of its aspirations as does Russia. In other countries there are more outlets for mental and moral energy, more dispersive areas consisting of comparatively free undertakings—political, commercial and even religious. Artzybashev's novel, Sanine, depicts the helplessness of Russian institutions to take up the shock and sorrow of dissipated political hopes. After the overthrow of revolutionary hopes in 1905 Russian youth could turn to sex adventure as the only recourse from the defeat of their social dreams.

Dostoevsky took his stand upon Russian nationality, in spite of the fact that he knew Russia was weak in its consciousness of nationality—indeed, that this was Russia's great weakness—"national consciousness is our weak spot."* He made Russia's unconscious national depths his gospel.

The peculiarities of Dostoevsky's subject matter are not only personal to him as an author, but also to the Russian people. They are more moved by pity than the rest of us; they are less the prey of social ambition and shibboliths; they are more open and unabashed at self-disclosures; they are less practical, more tolerant, easygoing, more "childish and crude," to use Dostoevsky's word. Gogol shows them so. Dostoevsky himself does the very things in Siberia, in Russia, Germany, Italy, that his characters might do.

*Letters, p. 152.

The life of the Russian people has been turned inward, like the life of India and Palestine, because in outward, natural directions, avenues of free advance were closed. If India had given birth to an Aristotle, it would not have produced a Buddha; if Palestine had yielded a Caesar, it would not have produced a Christ. Without the outlet of science or of politics, the soul has to satisfy its hunger by feeding upon itself.

So in Russian literature we find the deep personal note together with profound confidence in the instincts of the people. Even Russian music has consciously become the servant of humanity. You feel this in Moussorgsky's Boris Godounov—in the religious ecstasy of the kneeling people while the knout snaps across their backs. Moussorgsky's dictum was: "To feed upon humanity is the whole problem of art." So Dostoevsky sounded the depths of national strangeness. "I have my own ideas about art," he said, "and it is this: What most people regard as fantastic and lacking in universality, I hold to be the inmost essence of truth. Arid observation of everyday trivialities I have long ceased to regard as realism—it is quite the reverse."

But already Dostoevsky had made this confidence in the people the basis of Russian development. ". . . . with the people lies our whole salvation." [The people were the sacred depository of the divine revelation.] In their personal religion they witnessed the coming of God to them. They are Oriental in their confidence in the inner life and in the presence of God among men. G. Lowes Dickinson noticed this similarity of religious attitude between Russia and India.

"But the Indian peasant does really believe that the true life is the spiritual life; he respects the saint more than any other man; and he regards the material world as 'unreal,' and all its cares and illusion. I have seen on the faces of poor Indians at religious functions an expression I have seen nowhere else, unless, perhaps, in Russian churches."

"Out of this common faith that God reveals himself to the people and that their burdens and humiliations, their patience and meekness are of a heavenly origin, has come the idea so much insisted on by Dostoevsky: that the mission of the Russian people is to reveal to our civilization the Russian Christ by means of the Orthodox church. "I am not quite sure", said Dostoevsky in a letter to Strachov, "that Danilevsky will dwell with sufficient emphasis upon what is the inmost essence and the ultimate destiny of the Russian nation: namely, that Russia must reveal to the world her own Russian Christ, whom as yet the peoples know not, and who is rooted in our native orthodox faith. There lies, as I believe, the inmost essence of our vast impending contribution to civilization, whereby we shall awaken the European peoples; there lies the inmost core of our exuberant and intense existence that it so be."*

*Letters, p. 176.

Dostoevsky could not be happy without his own Russia around him. More unbearable than his exile in Siberia was his exile in Germany and Italy. Even in the land of the orange and myrtle, in Italy, a second birth-place to Goethe, to Browning and to many another nordic Dostoevsky was homesick.

"I cannot understand the Russian abroad. Even though there is a wonderful sky here, and though there are—as, for example, in Florence—literally unimaginable and incredible marvels of art, there are lacking many advantages which even in Siberia, as soon as I left the prison, made themselves evident to me: I mean, especially, home and the Russians, without which and whom I cannot live."*

Perhaps even this Russian national consciousness, which Dostoevsky introduces us to, or tries to develop, is, to some extent, a proud reaction against Europe. The same process is going on in Japan and America. After contact with more advanced nations, which develops admiration for them there is a rebound. Imitation is succeeded by aggressive nationalism. Japan became European after its revolution, then turned to an intensely Japanese culture. We in America do not care so much as we did in the middle of the 19th Century what Europe thinks of us. New nations, after their first foreign hero worship, choose self-sufficient ideals peculiar to themselves.

*Letters, p. 161.

Dostoevsky ignored the effect of the very thing he wished to preserve—the effect of the old Russian ways, faith, monasteries, deep-rooted superstitions—the things that make Russia homelike to a Russian. He was a fish out of water when out of his native country; yet oddly enough he did not admit the salutary advantage of environment, the influence of institutions, the value of improved social and political machinery as contributions to human progress. In short, Dostoevsky was a good psychologist but a poor sociologist.

IV

Dostoevsky's greatest work, if one consider the importance of the theme and the symmetry of execution, is "Crime and Punishment." A student in St. Petersburg without resources to continue his studies, and out of conceit with the usual student method of raising funds by teaching and by translation, conceives the idea that it is permissible for him—in fact, that it will ally him with the great and masterful characters in history—to murder an old woman pawnbroker and use her property as a pedestal of future service and distinction. This monstrous theory is fed by his poverty and at last masters him. The terrible deed is done, but it is contrived so clumsily that it involves a second unpremeditated murder and the letting loose of a cloud of furies. The Russian police; the law officers of the government; the searchings of his own conscience; his intolerable relations to his

friends, even to his own family, drive him to the preci
pice of madness.

Around him, too, is a constellation of unhappy lives.
A drunken Marmeladov, a sensualist Svidrigailov, and
the most lovely of all his creations, a child with the
Yellow Ticket, Sonia, who had gone on the streets to
keep the roof over the head of her drunken father, her
half-crazed mother and the smaller children. How much
Dostoevsky himself cared for Sonia may be guessed by
the fact that two years later he gave his own daughter
that name.

The mental struggles of the murderer to escape the
toils of the law; the misunderstandings of those who love
him; his incomprehensible behavior; the machinations of
his enemies, form a mass of incidents, mental, emotional,
conversational, of matchless intensity. The psychological solution is reached before the dramatic denoue-
ment in court. In the course of the relations of Raskolnikoff with Sonia, he makes a confession to her which
draws from the child a world of atoning direction and
consolation. That Sonia follows Raskolnikoff to Siberia
is merely an epilogue of what already for the central
figures is a completed drama.

"The Idiot," strange as it may seem from the title, is
perhaps the most agreeable of Dostoevsky's work. This
is owing to the charm of the character of Prince Myshkin
and to the attractiveness of the women in the story.
But the book is not so well balanced, as "Crime and

Punishment." Some parts while always showing careful—in fact, masterly development of scene and character —are spun out in a lengthy fashion that forgets symmetry and worse still, wearies the reader.

Dostoevsky evidently had for the character Myshkin well-founded personal sympathy and affection. Like himself, this hero was an epileptic who for most of his youth had been in the care of a doctor in Switzerland. At the age of twenty-six or twenty-seven he returns in pretty good physical and mental condition to St. Petersburg, to find out about an inheritance (which is kept for some time in the background of the story) and to connect himself with the life of his country to which in spirit he is enthusiastically attached. Immediately upon his arrival in the capital he introduces himself to a distinguished family believing that there was a blood-tie between them. The three handsome daughters of this family contribute many attractive chapters. But Prince Myshkin's adventure with a woman, a sufferer from her girlhood from the attentions of her guardian, who now wished to be free of this entanglement with his ward, and to marry suitably, is the explosive power of the story. The book, in fact, consists of a series of duels or personal encounters—they can hardly be said to be love affairs, they are so tempestuous and tragic. The men are "The Idiot" Prince Myshkin and Rogozhin—a passionate and half-educated young man, the inheritor of a large fortune from rich peasant ancestors. The women are Nastasya Filipovna, the unhappy ward, and Aglaia Epanchin, one of the three daughters of the Prince's relative. Out of furious encounters stalks nothing but tragedy. Nastasya is murdered by Rogozhin, who in turn is sent to Siberia. Myshkin is self-exiled from his beloved Russia in the custody of his Swiss doctor and degenerated into sheer idiocy. Aglaia marries a worthless Polish adventurer. "The Idiot" is abyssmal tragedy!

"The Brothers Karamazov" is the story of four men of widely different temperaments, the children of an inextinguishable sensualist, by three mothers, one being the vagrant idiot girl of the village. The reaction of these four natures against that of their father, which results in his murder at the hands of the child of the idiot girl, acquiesced in and almost suggested by his most intellectual son, and for which the one most like him is convicted and sent to Siberia; while the saintly Alyosha plays over the scene like a benignant spirit, forms the body of the story. In the background is a Russian monastery. Dostoevsky knew these well. He ran in and out of them as a boy. He liked them all his life and gives a beautiful picture of the spirit of the guiding intelligence in these monastic groups and of their benefactions to the Russian people. "The Brothers Karamazov" loses the momentum of its tremendous initial interest before the end of the story, which naturally slackens after the suicide of the real murderer. The analyses that follow matter little to a reader unless he is fond as Dostoevsky is of pulling apart and putting on the table the different parts of the workings of the human mind. Perhaps the author would say that the closing chapters of "The Brothers Karamazov" gave him the opportunity to call attention to the follies and mistakes of the Russian judicial system, and the ease with which justice miscarries.

Having himself been a victim of this system, he possibly was particularly anxious to depict it.

"The Possessed" is the most diffuse of his larger works—the least justified too in its theme—which at bottom is an attack upon the Russian reformers, whom he egregiously belittles. The book is a profuse illustration of a remark in one of Dostoevsky's letters: "Nihilism isn't worth talking about. Only wait until this scum that has cut itself adrift from Russia is quite played-out."*

Readers of Dostoevsky finish his novels with certain commanding scenes burned into their brains. In "Crimes and Punishment" it is a scene between Raskolnikoff and Sonia, in her chamber, when seated upon her bed he confesses his crime and she reads him the New Testament story of the resurrection of Lazarus. I know nothing in literature more inspired. In "The Idiot" it is a scene where Nastasia on her birthday, under the guise of a birthday party, calls to her home some of the

*Letters, p. 192.

men who are closest to her life and tries to settle their various demands, expressed or understood. One of them (her guardian) wishes to be free of her that he may make a distinguished marriage and settle down. One wishes to marry her to secure protection and promotion in business. Another passionately desires her and puts in her hand 100,000 rubles to bind the bargain. She throws the package into the log fire. In the midst of all this thunderous and sulphurous clearing of the air, the woman herself goes mad. To meet the consummate need of her poor, broken soul, the need of an honorable friend, Prince Myshkin "The Idiot" offers to marry her. These elements of the scene, taken together with the background of Russian customs and with the power of cumulative effect that Dostoevsky is master of, produces an overwhelming situation—an explosion in the life of each character.

In "The Brothers Karamazov" the extraordinary scene is between the child of the idiot girl and the intellectual brother, in which their two brains almost subconsciously fit into each other, with suggestions which are hardly expressed but understood, and lead to the murder of the father by the bastard boy.

In "The Possessed." it is the attempt of the charlatan leader of the people, Pete, to save his face, and perhaps his life, by securing from Kisseleff a promise of suicide which will free him from the terrors of discovery and punishment. When, however, the horrified follower from whom so much is expected, refused to make good his promise to kill himself, he is murdered by his chief.

All of these situations are cumulative creations in which extraordinary passions meet at a given point. They are not simple but complex activities which express a reaction of mind and feeling and are not dependent only upon outer incidents. In Dostoevsky, while his action so often inspires terror, his crises are psychological and not melodramatic.

Perhaps it is outside of his greater works, whose size seems to match their greatness, that Dostoevsky's quality is most masterfully seen. Take for instance, the matchless psychological study in his "Letters from the Under-World." A man of forty-one, who feels the sting of many humiliations of failures, is attracted by a girl of about sixteen, who comes to his pawnbroking establishment time and time again, to get rid of trifles which he sees show the depth of her poverty. She even tries by advertising in newspapers to find a position as governess or companion, and finally in desperation offers to do the most menial work. She is living with some aunts of semi-respectability. These our pawnbroker approaches with an offer of marriage to the child.

In spite of their differences in age and temperament, her sense of gratitude at first leads her to express affection for her husband and to delight in their new life. But his theory of her subordination to him; of her proper worship and devotion to him; his stern discipline and mean economies, little by little strip away her childish brightness and destroy her gratitude. Her tortures at his hand arouse her to intrigue; but she is too pure to suffer from so false a position or to permit its consummation. Maddened continually by his inexplicable moods, she tries to summon the courage to shoot him. We see him lying on the sofa, pretending to sleep, while she plays about his face with the cold barrel of a revolver. This is the memorable scene of the little story, but the end is too piteous—her leap from the window, clutching her poor icons—the pictured promise of something kinder than the hard heart of man.

In telling this story the husband does not use his wife's name (so we cannot recall her by her name). He is silent like those worshippers of a God who dared not call out the designation of their supreme divinity.

V.

You may not feel intimate with Dostoevsky's characters, as you perhaps do with those of Dickens or Thackeray, but you know them as you know no other persons in fiction—almost as the Judgment Day will know them. Possibly this is not the true comparison, this difference in our knowledge of the characters in English fiction and in Russian. The difference in our experiences may lie in psychological depth. The Russians seem emotionally richer than other Europeans. What we take to be greater workmanship in the Russian novelists—especially Dostoevsky—may in part be a discovery of richer material in the inner life of the Russian people. All his heroes are powerful natures, broken by wrong thinking or by trifling with action.

We may not feel the intimacy with Dostoevsky's characters that we do with the creations of other novelists, for the reason that they elude us as if in the hands of fate. The tragedy of Dostoevsky's work is not at the end but to be felt every moment in the escaping consummation of his personages,—their elusiveness, their instability, not so much of personal fortune as of personal determination. The fatefulness of character; the reaction of natures upon each other; the spiritual outcome of action and conviction,—all these exercise such a control over his thronging people that you know them with the vividness of a dream, but can just as little draw near or touch them.

The Heraclitean philosophy of πάντα ῥεῖ, that his opponent, Nietzsche, made much of, Dostoevsky exhibits in the shifting scenes of the inner life which bear all his creations away and out of reach with almost a Greek sense of fate—but one that proceeds not from without but from within. All things flow in the pages of Dostoevsky and escape into darkness in a fashion that leaves no room for laughter or tears, but only for eternal terrors or eternal hopes. In a book of Dostoevsky's you seem to stand upon the Styx with Charon, and to be allowed to watch (before your turn comes) the passage ot restless shades across into the eternities of judgment.

I have said that Dostoevsky was a good psychologist but a poor sociologist. He is a wizard in his knowledge of the inner workings of the soul, but he is a child in his knowledge of the workings of social institutions. He ignores the philosophy of history and what we can learn from a study of institutions; he ignores the power of predominating environment; he is not interested in economics. Man's history to him is only inner and seems to proceed unerringly under one set of institutions as another; under one economic theory as another; under a czar as under a democracy; under serfdom as under freedom. But what becomes of his motifs if Russia were a different sort of country. If it had a financial provision for poor students such as America has, there would have been no "Crime and Punishment." If Russia did not permit idiot girls to run loose and unprotected in its villages, there would have been no Karamazov Brothers. Without its rigid class system, there would have been neither "The Idiot" nor "The Possessed." His themes after all are temporary not eternal and are given him by circumstances not the soul.

Dostoevsky's traits are more Oriental than Occidental. Ethnologists tell us that the Russians are not Asiatics but Aryans with Tartar and Mongol groups. But the mysticism of Dostoevsky and its contentment with conditions; the asceticism of Tolstoi and its nonresistance are Asiatic not European. These traits of thought are peculiarly Oriental;—the tidelessness of destiny; the undifferentiated centuries; the indifference to conditions; the fear of desire; the dread of change; the unwillingness to see man's hand consciously at work in constructive evolution of social life. All these attitudes belong more to the East than to the West.

Dostoevsky is a revivalist not a revolutionist. He questions no fundamentals. His range of ideas is not wide He is intense not broad. He does not awake you to a new social view as Bernard Shaw continually does; but he arouses you to a new view of yourself and your own action. This is the function of the saint;—this purification of the heart on the basis of the received standards, as if these standards were final.

I do not know an institution that Dostoevsky questioned. He certainly made sincere submission to Russian autocracy; he fell in love with the Holy Synod; he believed in the Bible, in Immortality, in monogamy, even in Siberia. In fact, he kissed the rod and gladly accepted everything passed out to him. He was interested in clarifying and utilizing the present status. He had not learned the strange lesson that discontent and an enlargement of our position in the world, are of the essence of spiritual progress. That activity, as well as contemplation, has salutary use in regulating the disorders of the soul and that outer struggle promotes inner growth.

The character in English literature which most puzzles

English critics and is most unlike the English nature, Hamlet, is the prototype of the Russian nature. The first time I saw The Karamazov Brothers was at the hands of Orleneff and Nazimova, who were acting in a theatre in the Bowery near Grand Street. I found myself seated just in front of Richard Watson Gilder and Mr. Cahan of the Jewish Daily Forward. As the play went on Mr. Cahan whispered to me explanations. I remember especially his insistence on the Hamlet-like quality of Russian character—its indecision in action. The trait is more Oriental than European. This type receives more pleasure from contemplating its weakness of will and want of action, than in starting the needed undertaking. This is a well-known psychological dissociation of personality. Dr. Hall Bernard, in his "Psychology of Insanity," quotes Amiel as another illustration. "I very soon discovered that it was simpler for me to give up a wish than to satisfy it. I have been ashamed to desire." What becomes of self-abnegation, pacificism, the killing of desire, and of passive obedience under this searching scrutiny of modern psychology? They are transformed into anemia, cowardice, indolence. Action, which today is a psychological cure for many distempers of the soul, would perish in the triumph of quietism.

Dostoevsky, while he denied the power of environment as against the power of the spirit, was himself dependent upon environment. In 1868 he wrote from

Milan: "I am only heavy-hearted, homesick and uncertain of my position; my debt, etc., deject me horribly. And besides, I have been so alienated from Russian life that I find it difficult, lacking fresh Russian impressions as I do, to write anything at all. Only think—for six months I haven't seen a single Russian newspaper."

Dostoevsky, who seems so incredibly fertile in imagination, had to write, it appears, with his eye on the object. His imagination depended upon the facts, upon what his eyes looked out upon. Yet he cared only for the inward.

He was a romantic realist although dealing with the inner life. He did not spin his story out of himself, but constructed it out of the life around him. He even went to the newspapers for facts and found there a great deal of his most telling material. With the imagination of Poe he had some of the methods of Zola.

How surprising then that one who was constantly looking outside himself to understand himself, in short, goes to the world to understand the soul, should not have cared more what sort of a world surrounded the soul. Why did he not care about Russia's exhibition of social and economic change?

Dostoevsky's emphasis upon the inward rather than the outward is not only the result of his genius, of his faith in spiritual things; of his devotion to a people denied large expression in institutions; it is also the result of his infirmity.

VI.

The abnormalities of Dostoevsky physically, should be noted because it may be a door for the understanding of his social obtuseness in the larger place of possible reconstruction, which furnishes the program of the Russian revolutionist. Dostoevsky had no faith in their program. He had masterly psychology; he had no sociology. How can such limitations exist in geniuses? We see this limitation in all specialists.

Dostoevsky's own problems were perversely personal —his epilepsy, his strange moods and diseased sensibilities. He naturally attributed an equally personal note to all. He could not see a normal advance of a healthfully-minded nationality, by means of discussion and reform. He could not see the disappearance of some of his passionate criminals with the extension of opportunity for free self-expression. He imputed his pathological problems to the whole of Russia. He recommended everyone to take the medicine that helped him in his own epilepsy. Like the doctor in the anecdote, he was master of the situation when his patient had fits and must first throw him into fits as the road to recovery.

"The fits of epilepsy are very striking occurrences, and appear, at first sight, to be *sui generis*, and to be like nothing else that occurs in the human body; but, upon careful study, other recurring crises are found to take place, which have at least this in common with epilepsy— that they are recurring crises. In the common epileptic fit, consciousness is lost, the patient suddenly falls sense-less and powerless; and while he is thus unconscious, the muscles of the whole body are convulsed for the space of some seconds, or of a minute or two. On the cessation of the convulsion, the patient is still senseless or comatose, and this coma gradually lightens into sleep, from which the patient at length awakes, or can be aroused. Of the time that he was senseless, of his fall, of his con-vulsions, he remembers nothing when he emerges from his sleep. This is the ordinary course of events; but it is subject to many variations." ("Crime and Insanity," Charles Mercier, pages 59–60.)

In addition to his epileptic attacks he had mysterious fears. "There was," he said, "a frightful fear of some-thing which I cannot define, of something which I cannot conceive, which does not exist, but which rises before me as a horrible, distorted, inexorable, and irrefutable fact." This habitual condition was so distressing that his epi-leptic attacks became the most comfortable moments of his life. "During these times," he wrote, "I experi-enced a sensation of happiness which does not exist in my ordinary condition and of which I cannot give you any idea." "You happy, well people," said he, according to Sophie Kovalevsky, "have no idea of the happiness which we poor epileptics experience a second before the attack. Mohammed certainly saw Paradise in an epi-leptic attack, for he had these attacks just as I have."

I have already pointed out how rigorously he analyzed the character of Raskolnikoff.

Dostoevsky's condition (concludes Ossip Lourié) never went as far as dementia, but the progressive weakening of his critical sense was undeniable. It is to this that we should look for the cause of all the contradictions with which his life and his works were filled. This certainly is one of the characteristics of the semi-insane.

Loygue, who has thoroughly studied the psychology of Dostoevsky, gives the following information regarding his heredity and the onset of the disease. One aunt had "a very weak memory without any strength of character or resolution. She was susceptible to every passing influence. She was afraid of devils."*

To his brother Michael, Dostoevsky wrote from Siberia: "I have received your letter. I am afraid that your attacks will become like mine." In his earliest years he had nocturnal terrors, and in his later childhood frequent hallucinations. A friend of Dostoevsky, in his youth, who had witnessed his attacks, has also stated to Melchoir de Vogüé that at this period he would fall in the street, frothing at the mouth."†

"That there is any relation between epilepsy and feeble-mindedness in a hereditary way, that is to say, that an epileptic person is more apt to have feeble-minded children, or vice versa, our data give little evidence

---

*The Semi-Insane, Joseph Grasset, translated by Smith E. Jelliffe, p. 197. †The same, p. 198.

beyond the fact that epilepsy seems often to indicate a neuropathic condition, and that in such families feeble-mindedness may appear."*

Orchorsky says that in Russia comparatively few of the insane are shut up. He computes that there are a hundred thousand insane persons at large in the community. Undoubtedly, many of these insane or semi-insane, living without restraint in Russian cities and villages, account for the number of suicides and other acts of violence, as well as for the nature of many of Dostoevsky's characters. It has been reckoned that Dostoevsky exhibits in his novels forty types of sick people. He not only accepts the view of moral responsibility for his defectives but he assigned especial value to the utterances of his simpletons.

While it is well understood that there is value to the intellect received from nervous disorders of a certain type, the idiot and defective are not in this class. Their condition is due to degenerate conditions in which no superior intellectual power can possibly rise.

In Shakespeare's time idiots were called "innocents," and it was believed they (like little children) were nearer to God, and peculiarly under his care. In other words, Dostoevsky's sympathy for a class of mental defectives, such as naturals and simpletons, is really evidence of the high regard in which they were held in olden times and the opinion at that time that they were mediums of truth.

*Feeble-Mindedness. Henry H. Goddard, p. 513.

Again, what becomes of Dostoevsky's mysticism, as supernatural intercourse with the divine, so largely his method of personal enlightenment. His confidence in the soul as the only force; his attention to the mysterious background of moral judgment in ignorant peasants; his loyalty to the traditional religious habits of the Russian people, produce his confidence in mystic revelation. But today mysticism itself is revealed to science as an intelligible method subject to psychic and social law. "Mysticism in its full historical meaning, is as much a slow accretion, a group product, as is art, or grammar or mathematics."*

"But the mystical experience itself as it bursts upon the soul is a unifying, fusing, intensifying inward event. It may not bring new facts, it may open no door to oracular communications, it may not be a gratuitous largesse of knowledge; but it enables a soul to SEE what it knows, to seize by a sudden insight the long results of the slow-footed experience, to get possession of regions of the self which are ordinarily beyond its hail; to fuse its truth with the heat of conviction and to flood its elemental beliefs with a new depth of feeling. This dynamic inward event is not dependent upon any peculiar stock of ideas and is not confined to what is usually called the purview of religion; it is the sudden transcendence of our usual fragmentary island of reality and the momentary dis-

*Harvard Theological Review, April, 1915, p. 165.

covery of the WHOLE to which we belong. We can best help our age toward a real revival of Mysticism as an elemental aspect of religious life, not by formulating an esoteric 'mystic way,' not by clinging to the outgrown metaphysic to which Mysticism has been allied, but by emphasizing the reality of mystical experience, by insisting on its healthy and normal character, and by indicating ways in which such dynamic experiences can be fostered and realized."*

The dissociation common in epilepsy may be a ground of intenser powers of concentration, of putting away the world, which distracts and prevents in most of us the emergence of great thought.

VII

Dostoevsky has to be treated as more than a great literary figure: he has to be taken as a European figure, a prophet with a religious method. What are we to say about his mysticism, his opposition to western ideas, his gospel of weakness?

So far as his mysticism was confidence in the depth of the soul, it can be accepted as permanently true. But his opposition to western ideas was ignorance of the philosophy of history and of theories of economics. One institution is better than another, one theory more serviceable. To ignore sociology and see no salvation through superior institutions is to be blind to the past

*Harvard Theological Review, April, 1915 — p. 165.

and to the economic revelation of the present. It is to deny the findings of modern psychology that the ethical is produced by the social.

My interest in Dostoevsky, beyond my delight in reading him, came from the challenge he hurled against modern Europe—against the use of force; the value of science; the Roman Church and Socialism. Opposed to these he set up the spiritual qualities of the Russian people—meekness, patience and pity—and believed that the Russian Church by using these would cure Europe's ills.

Strangely enough we of today have just seen a battle royal between the opposing principles of Dostoevsky and Nietzsche—between the crucified man and the superman. At the present moment the superman has been laid low and the meekness and the patience of the Russian people have been the wonder of the world—in their successful political revolution; in their intrepid warding off of England, America, Poland and France,—and eastern allies, and in their tremendous effort to organize a form of economic life more brotherly than capitalism.

If the will to power has worked so badly that its protagonist, a former emperor, is a prisoner, the world may now give an opportunity to Dostoevsky's ideal—the power of meekness. Dostoevsky believes that the world is to be saved by the Christ of the Russian people, not by a hierarchy but by the living figure of patience, humility, meekness and pity. We have seen that the Russian people are particularly gifted with these qualities. We have seen that they themselves believe they are appointed to change and save Europe, while Europe and America have been afraid that this Russian program might be carried out.

In this very September, 1922, the Russian people announce that they do not believe in force and will not go to war against the Turks; so Dostoevsky's theory has become our practical problem.

Professor Carver, of Harvard College, has said something highly illuminating about meekness. He says that meekness is "teachableness." The most teachable nation will be the victorious nation. As for humility, it is a condition of teachableness. These two misunderstood Christian qualities must always go together. With them always will go piteousness, or a perception of the handicap under which millions of lives are lived.

There is no question that the two great wishes of humanity are for physical health and for financial security. The religion of the Russian people is at present based on financial security. The Russian sects which are in revolt from the orthodox church, have been strongly on the side of the revolutionary movement. When economics and mysticism join it is very likely we shall see extraordinary and creative results. Events seem to have justified Dostoevsky's greatest prophecy.

The Elegiac Tone in Sculpture

AT the unveiling of the monument to General Joe Hooker, in Boston some years ago, another famous general of the Civil War, General Dan Sickles, fell into conversation with a friend of mine, about St. Gaudens' statue of General Sherman, which stands at the main entrance of New York's great park. "I do not like it," General Sickles cried out, "It's senseless." "What's that woman doing under the horse's feet? She shouldn't be there."

From Paris comes a similar complaint of Bouchier's statue of Renan. "The figure of Renan, which ought to stand forth in great prominence" the critic claims, "is secondary to that of the goddess of reason. This draws the spectator's attention away from the philosopher commemorated by the statue."

The Boston Committee charged with the securing of a monument to Colonel Robert Shaw, got it into their heads, some twelve years after the order was given, that the bas relief was completed, they accordingly asked that it be put in place immediately. To their astonishment they received word from St. Gaudens that he wished to place above the marching negro soldiers and their white leader, an angel of death, moving with the troop—in fact, he was at that time modelling the angel. The committee replied, "We don't want an angel of death." Nevertheless they got one. Well worth working for and even a wrangle; for it was modeled from a lady who had the finest head, St. Gaudens told me, he had ever seen.

When I was a boy I heard of a sculptor who had been commissioned to make a statue of President Garfield. His first sketch, drawn soon after the tragedy, offered an heroic figure of the martyr president with a female figure that stood below the top of the pedestal, holding up a wreath or a bunch of palm. As time went on and the design was not executed, it changed. In each new sketch Garfield became smaller and the female figure arger: history and personal interest decreased; allegory increased. The last time I heard of this monument it was to contain a shield, inscribed with the name of the historical personage, embraced by the arm of an heroic Fame. This diminuendo of the fact and crescendo of the fancy struck me, at the time, as outrageously funny. Now, to maturer thought, it seems to me eminently suitable. Having been done by a great sculptor the memorial was probably deeply elegiac and beautiful.

In the following pages I am pleading for emotional sculpture.

Aristotle's dictum should not be forgotten—that a work of art should not be a symbol that is a sign by which one knows or infers a thing, but a representation—that is the thing itself. Yet the work of art may require the use of symbols to become a representation, especially a representation of deep moods and emotions. The use of symbols and of other indirect means to heighten the story sculpture tells, is the particular subject of this paper.

The popular attitude toward sculpture is more ignorant and open-mouthed than toward any other art. In this feeling of awe and easy admiration for the image of man and beast, shaped in clay or stone or bronze, is there not a reminiscence of old idolatries? Our ancestors' crude wonder, in their pagan period, at the rounded shape of the idol, and at its marvellous power, must explain, to some extent, our atavistic pleasure in the monstrosities that fill our squares. How, otherwise, could we endure the senseless, kindergarten modelling that we pay for and proudly place in conspicuous positions.

We can apply to ourselves, but with a difference, what Tacitus said about the stolid Roman attitude towards Greek art. "One having looked at a statue or a picture once, goes away satisfied, and never returns again." This lack of intelligence toward sculpture is unfortunate, because sculpture is the first art to be used in our streets for purely decorative purposes.

We cannot excuse ourselves, as the English do for their bad sculpture, who admit that they are not an artistic people. America is sufficiently infused with other than Anglo-Saxon blood to be looked to for artistic insight.

Two moods impel the erection of memorials to the dead: a desire to perpetuate a name in order to extend a knowledge of its virtues and its services or else a desire to express personal grief. These two moods meet in most monuments, which set forth both the worth of the dead and the grief of the living. To some extent these must always go together. The greater the beauty hidden by the tomb, the greater the mourning; the deeper the sorrows of the living, the more remarkable the onlooker must esteem those to have been for whom grief is shown.

But while commemoration and mourning are naturally united in funeral memorials—the great monuments to the dead emphasize one or the other. Either commemoration is the prime intention, or the exhibition of sorrow. Commemoration is the commoner use. Head-stones, lettered shafts, smoothed-off boulders, tombs, figures of Hope, Peace, the various Christian symbols— the cross, the anchor, the lamb—and sculptured like-nesses are used primarily for the purpose of commemoration, the decoration or departure from a simple inscription being expected to call attention to the name and so give it a larger and longer memory. We already understand this commemorative use of sculpture; our cemeteries are full of columns, urns and symbolic figures;

our public places hold portrait statues to remind the future of persons of wealth or worth.

In the silent memorial the dumbness of sorrow gesticulates as if there were no voice for sorrow that could sound from the tomb itself. But all bereavement is not as willing as Mrs. Browning to leave its stones mute:

> "Deep-hearted man, express
> Grief for thy Dead in silence like to death;
> Most like a monumental statue set
> In everlasting watch and moveless woe,
> Till itself crumble to the dust beneath.
> Touch it: the marble eyelids are not wet—
> If it could weep, it could arise and go."
>
> E. B. Browning, Sonnets from the Portugese.

The unvisited church-yard set with chiseled stone, abused by the elements, has seemed to compose a formal and soon-forgotten memorial. Literature has prided itself on its superior power to conquer immortality:

> "But you shall shine more bright in their contents
> Than unswept stone, besmeared with sluttish time.
> When wasteful war shall statues overturn,
> And broils root out the work of masonry."
>
> Shakespeare's Sonnet 55.

Stone has other uses than silent guardianship; it can throb with emotion and convey feeling as poignantly as poetry—yes, as searching as music. This grief made musical in marble, we do not often find, so we do not easily understand the elegy in stone. Grief speaking in sculpture is more than a commemorative symbol, a name prolonged; it is a poem visible and enduring, of the deepest emotions of human nature. With this perpetual sorrow,—with what may be called the elegiac tone in sculpture, we are little acquainted. The elegiac tone is as if the sculptor said to sorrow,

> "Once held in holy passion, still
> Forget thyself in marble."
>
> Il Penseroso.

The note of elegy is interpretative. The spectator as he gazes at a ludicrous lump of bronze, inscribed with a distinguished name, is no longer forced to be his own poet, he is no longer left to envelop it with whatever the name evokes in a sympathetic and intelligent observer—the benevolence, the genius, the tragedy —the sculptor, if he has the elegiac tone, has already explained the meaning of his statue in its composition; he has carved an elegy.

Hardly a city or town in America is without a soldiers' or a sailors' monument. But how crude, how unsuggestive, how purely commemorative their stereotyped structure! If you see one, you see all. A shaft of granite, against one side is backed a bronze soldier and, if the committee was in funds, against the opposite side

[134]

a bronze sailor. On the two remaining sides are heaps of cannon-balls. An ample, granite base supports this symbol of war. Stacked muskets, mortars, old cannon, bronze stars, eagles, etc., vary but do not improve the usual design.

War should say to sculpture what Benvenuto Cellini said to a rival sculptor, Bandinelli, who upbraided him for his murders. "At any rate, the men I have killed do not shame me as much as your bad statues shame you, for the earth covers my victims, whereas yours are exposed to the view of the world."*

For instance, a war waged for such ends as that of 1861 deserved poetic treatment. The preservation of a republic and the abolition of slavery are both epic themes. No such mighty political event associated with such spiritual passion, had happened before. An epoch like our Civil War in its monumental commemoration should have found expression in the most moving elegy.

"Full of stately repose and lordly delight of the dead."

Commemorative sculpture which illustrates, poetically a great life, and its eclipse by death, is not confined in its appropriateness, to the heroes of the battlefield or sea-fight. But war stirs the imagination and emotions more deeply than do the events of peace; and the veterans, marvellously escaped from the jaws of death, commemorate their own valor in honoring their dead companions.

---

*Symond's Introduction to Benvenuto Cellini's Life, p. 38.

Our numerous monuments to soldiers, sailors, generals, admirals have, at any rate, one important justification. They call attention to a hero's death which in war times cannot be given prolonged or earnest attention. A soldier falls in battle and his very companions, who are in similar peril, must press on and leave him behind, must forget the horror at their side. Even in times of peace we do not attend with deep thought and feeling to the mysteries and sanctities of death. Yet often the most dignified expression assumed by the human face comes at death. This transient nobility we must not spoil by our indignities; we must give death its due, and interpret death's transformations in lasting memorials.

The heroism of life and its inscrutable value; the loss and its eternal threnody are often recognized long after the event. Much of our best feeling about life is post-mortem. Death produces the pang and compels us to comprehend. Let us hasten, as soon as we make our discovery, to embody what so inexorable, so cruel a school-master has taught. Let us pile stone upon stone to commemorate our vision of life and death, whenever it is revealed to us. If death cannot be moved by our entreaty, we may still put into enduring form our tearful prayer.

The elegiac or poetic treatment of the military hero in sculpture is, consequently, truer to our enkindled thought and feeling than a purely realistic, or a purely romantic treatment. Generals with plumed hats, on rocking horses, pawing the air, like the General Jackson, in Washington, have about as much significance as symbols of war, as the candy figures of Bride and Groom on Wedding cake impart as symbols of marriage.

War is more than a conflict of lusty champions; the result is more than power and fame. War is the appeal of spiritual being to the arbitrament of force and the judgment of death. An intensely spiritual motive provoked the greatest conflicts, wars of independence, wars to repel invasion, or to right wrong. Such conflicts cry out that there are things more precious than life, which alone preserve for the race its desire to live, self-respect, honor, independence. For the motives of most wars are to procure or protect these spiritual states. So war is a strange paradox, a losing of life by those seeking life; a using of hate by those protecting love; a brutal appeal to force and physical destruction by creatures whose distinction it is that they have souls. War deals, then, with the mysterious borderland of existence where the living cross to be among the dead and where the spiritual also crosses to be with the animal, where progress is made by temporary retreat.

But if war is, indeed, a spiritual array—it is not enough that a great general in bronze should look like a swash-buckler, as does Colleoni; or that he should appear to be a mere mover of the machinery of battles, as does Marcus Aurelius on the Capitoline. In a great military statue there should be a contradiction. It should appear that the hero is not a self-satisfied butcher, or a vain-glorious poseur, but that he is lead by divine necessity, flint only for human need, and as if he saw dimly, through blood, a higher order and a moral victory reached by the road of his fearful carnage and social havoc.

St. Gaudens has grasped this paradox in his "Sherman." The man who said "War is Hell" must look it, yet not as a saint would look, but modified by a courage that had appealed to hell to right a wrong. The statue must tell us, however, that this grim-faced, tender soul's ordeal is ended. The face shows the man confronting war—its horror and its hope—but could express no more. There is a limit to the suggestive power of an expression. So by his horse's head moves Victory with her palm; she is wreathed and smiling; she holds up a commanding arm, bidding war to cease, bidding hell make way for heaven, rebellion for reunion, the battle-field for home and productive toil.

The elegiac tone in sculpture is a note of the great periods. Nothing in sculpture is more emotional than the class to which belong the bas-reliefs from the streets of tombs in Athens, the tomb of Ilaria del Caretto by della Quercia. Michael Angelo's Pietà, St. Gaudens' "Shaw," French's Milman, Cordova's tomb in Vienna, and Shelley's monument at Oxford.

The elegy in sculpture to affect us most strongly should be sung by one whom the observer can recognize as having grief-stricken relations with the dead, or by one who can naturally exhibit grief. On the Greek tombs, relatives appear in the act of bidding farewell, or in mournful attitudes, gods are represented who are messengers of death;—all of these are most somber.

So natural was the need among the Greeks of a perennial mourner, that on many tombs little, floating figures were sculptured called "sirens," symbols of perpetual woe.

There is a singular restraint about the figures on the funeral monuments of Athens—a restraint of fate. The marble men and women stand before us in a thoroughly human pose, but they look helpless. They exhibit the tenderest relations, but cannot carry out their will. There is a strange inanition, quite independent of the lifeless stone, but to be discovered in the inexorable difference of spheres, that terrorizes the beholder like motionless eagerness and paralytic dread in nightmare. To us, the living ones, Hades is visible, but no message can pass. Minds are bursting, hearts are breaking to show emotion, but no sign can be signalled, even so much as by a wrinkled brow. This is the excess of woe. The living unable to communicate with the dead; the dead unable to signal the living. The Athenian tombs represent, marvellously, this state of tension in death— the horror of human separation, the torment of love torn asunder. A clasped hand, a drooping head, a crouched body is instinct with eternal, unutterable pain.

The Greco-Roman period was lavish in sarcophagi,

but they exhibit little trace of that deep, poetic feeling about death—that sorrow we see in the elegiac examples of the great periods. These sarcophagi are more ornamental than funereal. They have bas-reliefs of bacchantes, of warriors, of Biblical subjects, which are, in fact, either purely decorative or else quite formal. Jonah, it may be thought, is used as a type of the resurrection, but other sacred subjects are used with no sorrowful significance.

In the Renaissance, the greatest elegiac subject is that of the dead Christ on His mother's knees, either alone or surrounded by those who loved Him. These kinsfolk, friends and disciples are most natural mourning figures.

No crucifix—that symbol of solitude—is as sad a sight as Michael Angelo's Pietà, in St. Peter's. Jesus lying dead upon the knees of His mother is the most sorrowful sight in marble. His mother's bowed head is a *miserere*. Yes, human sorrow, to be sure, but what other sorrow do we know? Is not human sorrow sad enough? Must we find a worse woe? Surely the mother's love gives highest interpretation to her Son's life. She prized and understood it, as even His followers did not. They called Him Master, but forsook Him, and in the end, this moment of Pietà, left Him to her again.

She cannot now gather her dead son to her in any tender caress—the frame of the man prevents; this is another element in her despair. Her right hand only half supports His shoulder and calls attention to her weakness. Maturity carried Him beyond her, then death; now she stares at both her enemies. Utter helplessness! Utter hopelessness! This was, for her, the end of affection, the end of her dream, the end of her own life, too, since a mother's life is in her son. Henceforth, her days are without expectation.

She is going over the past. She can see Him an infant lying on her knees, alive—so alive, and needing her care—such great care—and responsive to every touch. Like Meleager's mother Althaea, her heart may well be saying:

"Son, first-born, fairest, O sweet mouth, O child sweet
     eyes,
That drew my life out through my suckling breast
That shone and clove mine heart through—O soft knees,
Clinging, O tender treading of soft feet . . ."*

Yes, Mary with the stiff, cold body of Christ upon her knees interprets His tragedy. He went from her side into life. Now a little while and a storm has thrown Him up out of the depths of man's passionate hatred and ignorance. A worthless thing to the world and a deserted leader, He is again left to her. "Whose sorrow is like unto my sorrow. . . ."

In the Medici monuments Michael Angelo used as

*Swinburne Atalanta in Calydon.

[141]

mourning motives powerful allegory—the precursor of the modern symbolic figures.

Night and day, twilight and dawn, are fundamental participants with death. Out of such inchoate forces issues man to a more conscious and rarer experience, but brief although illuminated; for threatening him continually are the same undeveloped or slumbering forces. Lorenzo and Guiliano dei Medici's attendant figures tell the story of man's momentary separation from the brute and unconscious world of matter; they pre-figure his mixed and imperfect nature. These titanic recumbent forms are neither messengers from Hades or genii, but beings of a middle sphere of the universe which are struggling in pangs with souls which would be born. They are in a sleep like that of winter, out of which spring bursts. The forces of nature that the Greeks worshipped with such simple acceptance of their perfect beauty, their maturity, their adequacy to all that man would ever think about earth's energies, or about the surrounding air, the stars, and the fastnesses of death, now after centuries of new, human striving, a Christian striving, were treated by the great Florentine as semi-conscious and almost witless forms, enormous but unawakened.

The contrast between the carved likeness of Lorenzo and Guiliano, noble but rather conventional, at any rate alive, and the huge figures of twilight and dawn, of night and day, strange to man's mental world, suggests, too, by reason of the space in creation that has been covered between the unconscious and the conscious forms of life—a struggle as of something that has been overcome both in the physical and the moral range. The warrior figures, after all, have subordinated, only for a time, these elemental forces which lie as though flung from their hands. The perplexing, and to spiritual intensity, the forbidding inertness of the marble titans in the Sacristy of San Lorenzo, tells the story of an endless birth and death; of an endless struggle consummated by a partial and brief victory. The rigid marble asserts an old philosophy that nothing is immutable, but that all things flow.

Today allegorical figures—death, victory, reason, genius—perform the function of the Greek chorus and explain the situation. It is, too, as if when the hero, or poet, were to be immortalized in art, his attending genius, that loveliness of fate or action that made his fame, emerged tangible beside him and filled the artist's eye with a second form which would not quit the side of the being it had guided and animated. So the genius still guards the life.

"—that celestial power, to whom the care
Of life and generations of all
That lives, perteines in charge particulare."*

Bouchier's statue of Renan, without the figure of Reason would be undignified and meaningless. A fat,

*Fairie Queene, Bk. 2, c. 12, 47.

old gentleman, sitting heavily, not to say gloomily, on a country road-side bench—a rough, stone-supported slab—wondering where he will go next. Cover Reason with your hand and see how dumpy and painful the pose. Renan, by himself, was not a fortunate subject for the sculptor; a block of marble had to be cut very little to render his contour. His mind, even in sculpture, must beautify his body; hence Reason, stately and noble. Moreover, the actual female figure carries the eye of the observer up and increases the impression of Renan's height. Reason not only elevated and ennobles the monumental mass but it interprets Renan's mood. His weariness is not despondence, nor an old man's misgivings about his career, when returning to his birthplace, he reviews in strained reverie the scenes of his simple childhood. The melancholy question that he puts to himself, as he sits on the rough, cold seat: "Is this all? Is this the end?" is answered by the confident figure who coaxes him out of his brooding retrospect, away from the years gone forever, the dead past, by holding up to him blossoms of the immortelle, which are better than fame's laurel wreath, or victory's palm, —for Reason's gifts are enduring as the eternal mind of God.

In St. Gaudens' "Colonel Shaw" the elegiac note would be lacking without the angel; the other figures alone might represent the review of a negro regiment, parading in front of the Massachusetts State House. I look at the bas-relief. My eyes first encounter the horse and rider: the one headstrong and ungovernable, powerful in his upward pulling of the bit; the other slight, small, almost insignificant. My eyes travel to the pouting faces of the black, bronze troops. I happen to know their story. Free themselves, they are returning to the south to help free their race. What a marvel of new manhood! The slave from the cotton field becoming himself a liberator.

But my curiosity goes beyond these realistic figures, and finds above them the mournful angel, with cypress, or is it laurel in her hand? Then the beauty of a deathless procession envelops them, and my eyes fill with tears. Yes, that floating figure tells the story. They are passing down the street for the last time; they are leaving home forever. The side-walk crowds, the cynical idlers in the club windows near by, the rigid officials on the steps of the State House opposite will see their faces no more. They are marching away from the real, the things they know, into the vision they only guess, but are willing to die for. They are marching—this proud horse, this frail rider, these stolid figures—out of life into eternity.

Elegiac sculpture commemorates not only the separation of the dead from the living, but also the cleaving asunder of those companions, the soul and the body. It therefore honors the body by material immortality, and naturally accompanies those great periods of civilization that most appreciate human life. The body is worthy of immortality; beauty deserves more tears, the divine demands more manifestation.

"But while we are thus plentifully feeding our souls, we must not neglect their companions.

"Who are they?

"Our bodies: are not they the soul's companions? I had rather call them so than instruments, habitations or sepulchres."*

Such was Erasmus' blending of spirit and matter; such were the higher religious conceptions of the Renaissance.

The human body in persons of great beauty, as Praxiteles shows us in his Hermes, has a power of mental, even of spiritual expression and not the countenance alone. Mind is not dependent upon the face for expression. Fine communicativeness is not isolated in the features. The face is not the only surface through which the spirit can shine, or thought be read. A similar expressiveness of states of mind and soul is found in highly developed and beautiful bodies.

Matter is being refined in every direction and spirit shines through. On a crisp, November day I once asked a Japanese rickshaw man, bare of arm and leg, if he were not cold. His reply was a Yankee's answer—another

*Erasmus, "The Religious Tract," Familiar Colloquies, 8, 187.

question: "Is your face cold?" "No," I answered. "Me all face," he laughed out. English nerve doctors are reported to have said that American faces are too expressive. But nothing can be too expressive, since expression is the effort of all life from the clod up.

Nature seems trying to be "all face," all expression and revelation. We assist nature's effort when we develop the body, and keep it strong, supple, adequate. To be ashamed of the body, or carelessly to let it become deformed or gross is to defeat an evidently divine intention—and is, consequently, immoral, irreligious. A heavy, coarse or brutal countenance we all recognize as a sign of moral decline; so is a body composed of degenerating tissue.

The French say that it is necessary to make sacrifices in order to be beautiful. Here, then, in cultivating personal beauty, is a direction for religious ascetic zeal.

"Nor hath God deigned to show Himself elsewhere
More than in human forms sublime."*

How free of responsibility we feel for the dead after their burial! True, masses are said in some churches—religious offerings which correspond to the rites, gifts, food provided in earlier days. But we no longer decorate and furnish the interior of the tomb, to make poor souls feel at home, and so to ease their restlessness. Our silence toward the dead is, perhaps, an evidence of faith

*Michael Angelo's Sonnet to Vittoria Colonna.

[147]

and of humility. But after having done this—what of living memories? Commemoration, worthy grief, emulation, good-speech—these we should render the dead. We must bring the spent life brightly back into our lives by means of the energy and symbolism of art.

Art confronts death with immortal beauty. Death, which to us means destruction, is answered by beauty, which to us means perfections:—not physical perfection only, but that which we name spiritual—it is so high, so elusive, so alluring. The invisible powers of death demand a life; the visible powers of love, reverence, admiration and fear demand beauty to replace the life, to commemorate it—beauty as being what the life was at heart, what it meant in the unseen harmonies of existence. So art is faith without creeds.

How crude, cruel, final is death. The brutal has triumphed. If it were not for art, tragedy would have the last word. But art takes the destructive fact and constructs a beautiful immortality, that living minds can brood, that living hearts can love or fear; that living lips can whisper, and that robs tragedy of its last, if silent, vindictiveness.

Human nature is not large enough to hold human calamity. The world overwhelmed by the most hideous condition of destruction the sun ever looked down upon, has become callous and more or less mechanical in its response, either to an enumeration of these horrors or to their amelioration. A woman can shed tears when her husband is put in the coffin. A child can weep at its mother's death. When worse individual misfortunes are multiplied by millions, there is no corresponding personal or social enhancement of grief.

Human nature must not produce greater calamity than it can mourn, or it will be destroyed by it.

On the contrary, human nature flies automatically to its own protection and coats itself with a superficial unconcern or it makes a spiritualistic appeal, in order that it may not likewise perish. This inability of human nature to arise to the highest form of sympathy or to develop feelings so profound as to destroy the one who feels, makes of life a one-window affair, from which little can be seen and guessed of the whole of existence.

Here we find a reason, too, for art because in the expression of art we have embodies the feelings of the individual as far as they can be felt, realized and expressed in the moment. For swathed, protected and hardened human nature, the deep meaning of life has to come from a thousand of these notes struck by art for the poet, the musician, the painter. So the world in its spread of consciousness grows to feel, what an individual cannot feel, of the waste and terrors of life. Indeed, these destructions have so much consumed his attention that he is not at home in joy and gladness. In music and poetry, joy and gladness are notoriously inadequately expressed. Tragedy is that in which art has distinguished itself;

just as the Crucifixion is the most popular art symbol of the Christian centuries.

Art loves to move along the borderland of life and death; its immortal works are like the monuments of Gettysburg that marks the space where men passed from life to death. So art illuminates life by showing it against the dark background of destruction and forgetfulness.

The Last of the Poets

"SOON, the last poet will offer to the Muses the last dove," said Jules Lemaitre. "Judging from all appearances there will be no more verse in the year 2000." Are we so rapidly approaching the death of an art? May it be possible that we ourselves know and foregather with the last poet the world will ever see; that we perchance dine and joke with the last of a line of royal beings—of a dynasty that for us began with Homer and contains the names of Sophocles, Virgil, Dante, Shakespeare and Goethe. Such an event as the end of poetry will be more marked in future history than the downfall of the Roman Empire. There have been many nations but few arts; for an art is a rarer and more final product than a nation. Le dernier poète, though he be a weakling, will be more significant than Odoacer's victim, Augustulus, the last Roman Emperor in It... more renowned than the last Constantine slain by ... torious Mussulmans, at the gates of Europe. What ... even to be a friend of the last poet!

Within the ranks of the literati there are ag... enemies of poetry who argue that its technique, *i...* up box of rhymes, assonances, etc., are att... primitive society, like an Indian's warpaint...

and indicate, when used today, a recession to a childish age. Among these traitors to literary traditions, Jules Lemaitre was the most confident spokesman.

"Le mouvement scientifique et critique qui emporte notre âge est, au fond, hostile aux poètes. Ils ont l'air d'enfants fourvoyés dans une société d'hommes. Comment perdue son temps à chercher des lignes qui riment ensemble et qui aient le même nombre de syllable, quand on peut s'exprimer en prose, et en prose nuancée précise, harmonieuse? Bon dans les cités primitives avant l'écriture quand les hommes s'amusaient de cette musique de language et que par elle ils gardaient dans leur mémoire les chose dignes d'etre retenues. Bon encore au temps de la science commençante et des premières tentatives sur l'inconnu. Mais depuis l'avènement des philologues. L'amour des cadences symétrique et des assonances régulière dans le language écrit est sans doute un cas j'atavisme . . . Bientôt le dernier poète offrira aux Muses la dernière colombe; suivant tout apparence, on ne fera plus de vers en l'an 2000."*

"There never was and never will be any reason," said Professor Tyrrell, "why thought should express itself in words which produce a certain assonance at certain intervals. Yet, as was said of dicing in ancient Rome, it will ever be forbidden and ever practiced."†

In the opinion of other members of the literary craft,

Jules Lemaitre on François Coppée in Les Contemporains, p. 83.
R. Y. Tyrrell, Latin Poetry, p. 307.

it is the imagination, the agent of poetry, that discredits it. This function of the mind, they claim, is most powerful in childhood and in the childhood of the race. An art is debased by so puerile an instrument.

Imagination being then the instrument of poetry, and children having a certain vivid use of that faculty, even Macaulay asserts that poetry must be at its best in a crude and childish age. "In a rude state of society men are children with a greater variety of ideas. It is, therefore, in such a state of society that we may expect to find the poetical temperament in its highest perception. In an enlightened age there will be much intelligence, much science, much philosophy, abundance of just classification and subtle analysis, abundance of wit and eloquence, abundance of verses and even of good ones, but little poetry."

In spite of the unfavorable prognosis of these doctors of letters, the true worshippers of the Muses, will pray that poetry may survive the year 2000. The death of poetry would darken the heavens permanently for many natures, not the most unpractical or passive or least in touch with their times. Mazzini, the embodiment of the struggle for freedom and nationality in the Nineteenth Century, loved poetry.

"We have exiled poetry from life, and enthusiasm and faith have gone with it, and love, as I understand love, and constancy in sacrifice, and the worship of great deeds and great men."* "To reveal ties and create affections is the business of poetry."†

But without trying to make out a great case for poetry; without invoking the threatened Muses in any lofty strain, cannot we refute the detractors of the art, even using their own rather mechanical terminology? Many of us must certainly know our own reasons for wishing Poetry well.

Poetry, at any rate, is meeting the test of our time—efficiency; it delivers the goods. Verses have accomplished jail deliverances that petitions, signed by eminent citizens and enforced by the arguments of shrewd attorneys—yes, even wet with the tears of woman's beseeching love—could not bring to pass. The New York Evening Post . . . was true to its character as a literary medium in preserving the following:—

"POEM SAVED CONVICT'S LIFE. GOVERNOR WEST SAYS HE WAS INFLUENCED BY 'THEY HUNG BILL JONES.'

"Salem, Ore., September 6, 1911, Frank L. Stanton's poem, 'They Hung Bill Jones' saved the life of Jesse P. Webb yesterday, according to Gov. Oswald West. Webb who had been convicted of the murder of William A. Johnson, a ranchman, instead of being hanged at noon, was the guest of honor at a convict dinner in the penitentiary."

*Bolton King's "Life of Mazzini," p. 313.
†Bolton King's "Life of Mazzini," p. 319.

"Special to the New York Times, Washington, July 10, 1912. Pres. Taft today released from prison a poet named Mary E. Brown, because she wrote a poem which appealed to soft emotions and the sense of rhythm."

The New York Times, Monday, March 22, 1920.

"Held up by poet robber. Rhymester with revolver takes $54 from bakery. The baking establishment was entered shortly after midnight by a young man who leveled a revolver at Kurtz, and said:

" 'Say, kid, just look me in the face
I just dropped in to clean this place.
So come across with all you've got—
I never fail to hit the spot.'

"Kurtz threw up his hands and the stranger, keeping the gun pointed with one hand, went through the cash register, taking therefrom $54, with the remark:

" 'I thank you for this wad of dough,
And now, good day, I think I'll blow!' "

Still another example of the Muses' help (New York Times, August 19, 1913):

"Pat Crowe, a western desperado, was freed by a Washington judge moved by an appeal ending:

" 'Not void of all ambition,
Nor dead to every wrong.

> And I did not wish to be alone.
> I would rather be where vultures rave
> And fulfill my earthly mission,
> Ere I find the quiet grave.' "

I commend the writing of poetry to all would-be criminals. Poetry is the plush-handled jimmy of jail deliverance.

After these examples of the success of jail-breaking jingles we may expect poetry to look up. The poet, so long a target for editorial humor, may in future be needed on law faculties, or may supersede criminal lawyers. Notorious gun-fighters hereafter may carry upon their person amulets, in the form of poems, to ward off vengeance of lynchers or the righteous sentences of misguided judges—in fact, calculated to wring pardon from mob or jury, from governors or presidents.

But why have poetry? Why should not poetry without more ado be ousted by prose? Cannot prose do everything? If Macaulay is right in saying that the deeper and more complex parts of human nature can be exhibited by words alone, if no other art—painting, sculpture, music—tells the whole story quite as aptly as words tell it, why not go about the matter sensibly and say what has to be said in a straightforward manner.*

Poetry has a recognized place, hard to destroy. Coleridge's distinction between prose and poetry is too for-

*Macaulay on Milton; Macaulay on Byron.

mal, "Prose consists of words in their best order, but poetry consists of the best words in their best order."* The terms "best words" is made to fill too large a breach. Matthew Arnold interprets Coleridge's phrase when he says—"Now poetry is nothing less than the most perfect speech of man, that in which he comes nearest to being able to utter the truth."† But is not poetry, we may ask, first a matter of thought and emotion before it is a matter of "best words" or "perfect speech?" When a theme is so emotional that it mounts into the region of imagination and is sustained and interpreted there, its oral, or written utterance (if it passes beyond eloquence) will be poetry. So Wordsworth calls poetry "the breath and finer spirit of all knowledge." Dr. Johnson was nearer the truth when he said that poetry perpetuated a language, because to read it you had to learn the language, since poetry could not be adequately translated.

The dispute as to whether imaginative prose is poetry cannot be settled on merely logical lines. Even if we must dare to challenge the opinion of Goethe who lays it down that a prose translation turns over to a reader the entire content of a poem. But the content of a poem is not the idea pure and simple or even the formulated thought. The content of a poem is rather the poet's lyric mood, a spiritual not a historical moment; an exaltation of feeling which demands expression in

*Table Talk.   †Essays in Art 2, p. 128.

one particular way and not in another. Not the history of ideas but of personality is involved.

Every art is an expression of a spiritual state. A poem translated into prose is not a transcript of that emotional state which required or even thought it required rhythm and rhyme.

Poetry's use of rhyme, rhythm, etc., is not *un cas d'atavisme*. The imagination being the instrument of poetry, does not make it out a childish performance. The best poetry is not the product of early civilization. In short, *la dernière colombe* will not be offered on the altar of the Muses in the year 2000. A literary intelligence which could throw out such a hazard utterly lacks the consciousness of what constitutes the incentive to poetic expression.

Dr. Johnson, we saw, judged that poetry preserved a language. Verse lost so much in translation that students, he was confident, would learn a language for its poetry who would not for its prose. But poetry can just as little be translated into prose of its own vernacular as into that of another tongue. If you doubt it, try your prentice hand at turning into English prose this song of William Blake:

"How sweet I roamed from field to field,
And tasted all a summer's pride,
Till I, the Prince of Love beheld
Who in the sunny beams did glide.

"He showed me lilies for my hair,
  And blushing roses for my brow,
He led me through his gardens fair
  Where all his golden pleasures grow.

"With sweet May-dews my wings were wet,
  And Phoebus fired my vocal rage,
He caught me in his silken net,
  And shut me in his golden cage.

"He loves to sit and hear me sing,
  And, laughing, sports and plays with me,
Then stretches out my golden wing,
  And mocks my loss of liberty."

Or this by Bliss Carman:

"She lives where the mountains go down to the sea,
    And river and tide confer,
Golden Rowan, in Menalowan,
    Was the name they gave to her.

"She had the soul no circumstance
    Can hurry or defer,
Golden Rowan, of Menalowan,
    How time stood still for her!

"Her playmates for their lovers grew,
    But that shy wanderer,
Golden Rowan, of Menalowan,
    Knew love was not for her.

"Hers was the love of wilding things;
　　To hear a squirrel chir
In the golden rowan, of Menalowan,
　　Was joy enough for her.

"She sleeps on the hill with the lonely sun,
　　Where in the days that were,
The golden rowan of Menalowan
　　So often shadowed her.

"The scarlet fruit will come to fill,
　　The scarlet spring to stir
The golden rowan, of Menalowan,
　　And wake no dream for her.

"Only the wind is over her grave,
　　For mourner and comforter,
And, 'The Golden Rowan, of Menalowan,'
　　Is all we know of her."

Or this by Gladys Cromwell:

"DELIVERANCE"

"Deliverance?　You mean this empty cup
　　My days keep filling up;
　　You mean my future into which keeps flowing
　　Forever without my knowing,
　　The irresistible current of my past?"

These poets' moods required rhythm for their expression and if the bare idea were offered in prose, a spiritual state would have been recorded falsely, a historical lie would have been perpetrated. Nor is this truth of a special art which, in any other sort, would be falsely rendered, a "truth of madness"; but truth immortal.

If rationality and nothing else, or if a procession of ideas alone were the object of life, you could accomplish this transformation—you could express in words or in formulas all the arts, and reduce them to equivalents in one art. You cannot do this. Phidias and Sophocles, Dante and Shakespeare are as stubborn as elemental forces in nature and refuse to shuffle places or to be merged into the art of Thucydides. Does this not mean that they record more than ideas of a historical progression. This *more* I take to be the spiritual warrant of personality, that which gives it value above the impersonal activities of mind and will. So art is the joyous self-expression of personality, and insists on those differentiations that characterize personality. The sacred precinct of poetry being personality, a region where wonders must be seen as the mystic sees with closed eyes, nothing but the imagination can behold its raptures and its vicissitudes—the labors of the soul. The master work in poetry, therefore, has been the imaginative creation of immortal men and women, Agamemnon, Antigone, Electra, Hamlet, Lear.

When we assert rather proudly that poetry is the work of the imagination, have we not delivered ourselves over to Macaulay and to Lemaitre? Decidedly not. The phrases, "Of all people children are most imagina-

[161]

tive," "The despotism of the imagination over uncultivated minds," do not accomplish what Macaulay supposed—the relegation of poetry to the nursery. Lemaitre's comparison of poets in the days of science to children straying into the society of grown-ups—"Ils (poetes) ont l'air d'enfants fourvoyés dans une société d'hommes"—does not put poets into a school for defectives, unless it be that fortunate company of "incurable children" in whose society Lowell expected gladly to end his days.

If the use of the imagination as a creative agent were to condemn poetry, the same argument would condemn every art, for imagination is the servant of all the Muses. When a painting or statue lacks imagination it is worthless. What would Praxiteles or Michael Angelo, Millet or Turner or Rodin have created without imagination?

Commerce, business and finance need imagination, not to speak of war. E. H. Harriman, for instance, was a dreamer, but by the creative power of his genius he made his dreams come true. Otto H. Kahn, in an interview on Operatic and Dramatic Art, said of Mr. Harriman: "He had a great poet's imagination but he rhymes in rails." The French say, "No imagination, no great general."

Science, itself, and consequently civilization, are under everlasting obligations to the imagination. Through that faculty those hypotheses are guessed at, which by subsequent investigation must be proved to be true.

Agassiz saw glaciers in Switzerland and dared to guess that Europe and America, ages ago, were nearly covered with ice. Think of this picture in his imagination never before dreamed of! But the uses of the scientific imagination are well known. "Disciplined imagination," says Karl Pearson, "has been at the bottom of all great scientific discovery."*

"Pasteur had vivid imaginative faculties," says his biographer, R. Vallery-Radot. "His great intuition, his imagination, which equalled any poet's, often carried him to a summit whence an immense horizon lay before him."

"Nowadays, the qualities we call real," according to Alfred Fouilles, "are no longer considered as anything but particular cases of what we call imaginary. What is a Pascal, or a Leibnitz; they see beyond all realities, and live in a kind of perpetual dream of the possible and see in physical phenomena but echoes of higher harmonies. Faraday compares his intuitions of scientific truth to 'inward illuminations,' ecstasies, as it were, raising him above himself. One day after long reflection on thought and matter, he suddenly saw in a poetic vision the whole world 'traversed by lines of force,' the infinite trembling of which produced light and heat throughout the immensities. And this instinctive vision was the origin of his theory."

Macaulay used another illustration to prove that imagination is a childish trait. "Poetry," he says,

*Karl Pearson, Grammar of Science, p. 11.

"produces an illusion on the eye of the man as a magic-lantern produces an illusion on the eye of the body and as the magic-lantern acts best in a dark room, poetry effects its purpose most completely in a dark age." He might just as well have said that because knowledge breaks in upon ignorance, therefore it may be expected to produce its greatest effect upon a fool. On the contrary it is the wise man who best appreciates the suggestiveness and forces of knowledge, and gets the most out of its new fact.

I question too whether the imagination is strongest in childhood. At that age it may have more undisciplined sway, when experience, reason, moral judgment have either not developed or lack material to occupy the mind. Strength of imagination is reserved for maturity and seems to mark the flowering of the faculties.

A necessary qualification for scientific investigation is that the experimenter should be "young in imagination." The scientific discoverers of the 19th century were largely made by young men. "Davy made his epochal experiment of melting ice by friction when he was a youth of twenty. Young was no older when he made his first communication to the Royal Society, and was in his twenty-seventh year when he first actively espoused the undulatory theory. Fresnel was twenty-six when he made his first important discoveries in the same field, and Arago, who at once became his champion, was then but two years his senior though for a decade he had been so famous that one involuntarily thinks of him as belonging to an older generation. Forges was under thirty when he discovered the polarization of heat, which pointed the way to Moht, then thirty-one, to the mechanical equivalent. Joule was twenty-two in 1840 when his great work was begun, and Mayer, whose discoveries date from the same year, was then twenty-six, which was also the age of Helmholtz when he published his independent discovery of the same law. William Thomson was a youth just past his majority when he came to the aid of Joule before the British Society, and but seven years older when he formulated his own doctrine of the dissipation of energy. And Calusius and Rankine, who are usually mentioned with Thomson as the great developers of thermo-dynamics, were both far advanced with their novel studies before they were thirty." Even when important discoveries are made by men advanced in years, it is largely on account of this youthfulness of imagination that they are able to outrun the fact presented to them and see theories, high generalizations, which at once include and explain these facts.

The loss of imagination in scientific employment or in old age does not invalidate the obligation of science to the imagination. Darwin lost his imagination in the course of his scientific studies. The members of the Royal Society and the Académie des Sciences are "for the most part possessed of non-visual memories."*

*Cf. Ribot, on Emotions, p. 16.

The lack of imagination is even a cause of deterioration of musical comedy. The lack of visualization is common among theatrical managers. The writer of an original libretto has about one chance out of fifty of having it accepted. Henry Blossom, after many disappointments, resolved never to waste time in writing an original opera libretto. He found managers positively unable to visualize the characters and episodes in an unacted play.*

But we must remember that the members of learned bodies are, for the most part, no longer young. Old men receive the honors; young men do the work.

This lack of imagination in distinguished old age can not be regarded as the *terminus ad quem* of high mental activity. Because these personages of earlier scientific activity and of prolonged scientific interests, disclose toward the end of their careers an absence of imagination, we may not argue that the loss of imagination is to be desired, any more than those other signs of old age are to be desired enumerated by Hamlet:

"The satirical rogue says here that old men have gray beards; that their faces are wrinkled; their eyes purging thick amber and plum tree gum and that they have a plentiful lack of wit together with most weak hams."

Hamlet, Act II.

The loss of imagination is closely connected with a

*R. C. Dasher, The Dearborn Independent, July 26, 1919, p. 7.

lack of visual memory. But a lack of visualizing power is a disadvantage, not an advantage. If the first step in knowledge is that of forming concepts from perceived data; if the next step is that of imaginative rearrangement of such concepts, and the final stage is that of reason and logic, we are not to infer that in consequence of this relativity in position, the earlier stages can be omitted; indeed, they are all required for the highest use of our faculties.

The imagination is not seen at its strongest in primitive literatures. In Japanese literature, for instance, "The Kojiki and Nihongi have preserved to us," says W. G. Ashton, "more than two hundred of these (early) poems." "Their study tends to correct ideas such as that of Macaulay, who, doubtless, reasoning from the now exploded premise that Homer is a primitive poet, argued that 'in a rude state of society we may expect to find the poetical temperament in its highest perfecting.' Judging from this early poetry of Japan, a want of culture by no means acts as a stimulus to the poetic faculty. We nowhere find 'the agony, the ecstasy, the plentitude of belief' which Macaulay would have us look for in this product of an age and country which were certainly less advanced than those of Homer in intellectual culture. Instead of passion, sublimity, and a vigorous imagination, we have little more than mild sentiment, word-plays and pretty conceits. Moreover, a suspicion will not be banished that even for such poetical qualities as they possess, these poems are in some degree indebted to the inspiration of China. Of this, however, I cannot offer any definite proof."*

The imagination has a psychologically creative use. It builds together early sensations, it is the cement of early psychic experience upon which memory is reared.

"Elle fait la beauté, la justice, et le bonheur, qui est le tout du monde. L'imagination dispose de tout." Pascal, *Pensées.*

The imagination and its products has educational value. "A man's character and mind," said Frederick Robertson, "are moulded for good or evil far more by the forces of imagination which surrounds his childhood than by any subsequent scientific training. The use of the imagination instead of reducing mature man to the status of a foolish child, develops the child into the man.†

So the fruits of poetry will nourish the maturing mind. "Education in the future," Stanley Hall feels sure, "will make great use of these children of the poet's imagination, for in them can be studied more easily than anywhere else types of character in their simplicity. The understanding of them even to the extent of dramatic representation, modern educators assert, will become a part of the school drill.‡

We may go farther and insist with Matthew Arnold that in the future knowledge will come, not first by way

*W. G. Ashton's "Japanese Literature," p. 9. †L. O. Brastow, "Representative Modern Preachers, p. 56. ‡Stanley Hall, "Adolescence" 11, 439.

of logic and scientific disquisition but through "the imaginative reason"—that swift logic of sympathy that knows the wisdom of the past and the future. The truth that slavery was wrong, that persecution for religious belief was wrong, that he who loses his life shall find it,—these truths were come at, not by syllogism but by imaginative reason. Poetry is not degraded because imagination is its instrument, but exalted through its dependence upon this noble function of the mind.

Finally the poet is likely to go far with William Blake, "The imagination is not a state, it is human existence itself."

But are the forms of poetry necessary—rhythm, rhyme, etc.? "But perhaps of poetry, as a mental operation," says Dr. Johnson, slashing Milton's verse "meter or music is no necessary adjunct." Why this "perhaps"? Meter is a necessary adjunct of poetry as a mental operation; at this very point lies the foundation and reason for the art of poetry.

The critics of poetry who belittle rhyme, rhythm, etc., do not know the findings of modern psychology; instead of being, as they suppose, ahead of their age, they are behind it. Music is essential to the poetic conception.

The human circulation itself is susceptible to rhythm. "Gretry has already noted that the pulse is sensitive to rhythm, and he has recorded several observations made on himself, showing that the pulsations are accelerated or retarded, according to the rhythm of a chant heard internally. This chant was not heard by the eye from notation; the rhythm, consequently, was that of ordinary verse when read to one's self; it was not a sensation received through the ear.*

In the brain, too, there is a rhythm at different times of the day or night which proceeds from the different degrees of sensibility to light, sound and temperature. These physiological rhythms are habits of organized activity which have been found advantageous, and which in men are highly developed."†

Rhythm has been shown by Professor Bucher ("Labor and Rhythm") to have been an essential force in construction civilization, by means of the unison of effort, in dances, marches and working songs. Armies march to a step, and the great weights, such as the stones of the pyramids, could only have been carried by a rhythmic-like step. In Japan I heard corn ground to songs. In Benares I saw great slabs of stone carried on several shoulders to a chanted step. "The rhythmical labor songs of harvesters from antiquity to the present time are expressions of the spirit of the group and are of the nature of genuine ceremonials."‡ "A well constructed phrase," said Flaubert, "adapts itself to the rhythm of respiration."

---

*Ribot—Psychology of the Emotions, p. 105.
†Donaldson, Growth of the Brain, p. 294.
‡Edward Scribner Ames, Psychology of Religious Experience, p. 114.

"The love of rhythm is," says Stanley Hall, "an accomplishment of adolescent changes. Declamation, music are then practiced and the rolling of sentences into cadenced periods. These practices seem to be calculated to cadence and harmonize the emotional nature. They have a constructive value."*

All life is rhythm from a psychologist's point of view. There are rhythmic processes of thought accompanying the birth of ideas which find their satisfaction and expression in given poetical and musical form. The Greek could feel the joy of the iambic and the sadness of the trochaic meter. Rhythm in itself has definite emotional effect.

A Rondel or a Spenserian stanza might be called a semi-ready coat for a certain kind of thought. These seemingly highly artificial products are, as a matter of fact, psychological discoveries. The sonnet-maker is not a foolish "carver of cherry-stones," but a house-hunter for a fussy idea.

But the knowledge of the technique of an art discloses methods of producing effects peculiar to the art. Even the prose writer is not without his rhetoric and his unrememberable names for figures of speech with which he strews his page. If he looks askance at poetry because it is not always spontaneous or extempore, he may be asked whose prose, if masterly, is spontaneous? Did not Flaubert "seek" the word—one word, sometimes

*See also Dr. W. A. White, Foundations of Psychiatry.

for a week? Did not Pater write on every other line of his ruled paper, so that he might fill in corrections and qualifications on the lines between? If poetry is an art, you have said all there is to say by way of complaint of artifice. Of course, it has its metier—but rather less worked out (if that is any merit) than several other arts. Nor is poetry cried down when proven to require longer incubation than prose. If art degenerate in proportion to the time it takes, what shall we say to a cathedral whose construction has outlasted generations? The mechanical difficulties of an art do not condemn it. Labor does not discredit a masterpiece. The length of time it took to build St. Peter's does not lessen our admiration.

The sterility of poetry in England during the last decade of the nineteenth and the first decade of the twentieth centuries, contains here and there a glint that suggested the possibility of restoration. New forms were being experimented with and in the masque and pageant, which were found convenient for teaching nationalization, socialization and surrounding the common things of life with more beauty, there appeared a natural place for lyrics which in directness of theme as well as application to a special occasion, gave a new reality to the most poetical form of verse—the song.

To these stirrings and developments has been added the revolutionary expression in verse of the followers of *vers libre*. Such a method has the argument of the classical tradition. Greeks and Latins did not care for rhyme. This is remarkable when it is remembered that they had languages with case endings which could have produced infinite numbers of rhymes. Possibly this ease and consequent monotony were the reasons why the Greeks and Romans did not cultivate rhyme.

The English language is particularly unsuitable to rhyme; but tradition has been strongly in favor of its use. The free verse inventors ran away from any other control or consideration than metrical expression of emotion or thought. This is a refreshing variation in English verse and will naturally bring into the field of poetic production hundreds of persons who had no gift or liking for the fetters of rhyme.

Outside of the whole question of rhyme and of its pleasure to the ear, free verse easily cultivates a more every day theme and deals with the common and average life of the world more naturally than the ornate traditional rhyming. Here again free verse clasps hands with democracy. Possibly the outcome will be a greater freedom in handling poetic subjects and a passing backward and forward between old forms and new, in the same poetic composition.

We cannot imagine a poetry which is divorced from music, and this means all manner of beautiful sounds that appeal to the ear. Even where the rhyme has been retained by our new poets, the versification of late has returned to the simple couplet which accentuates rhyme and form.

At any rate, poetry was never on the threshold of larger hopes than today. Poetry has cleaned house in the matter of technique, ideals and subject-matter; it is now ready for great work. The year 2000 instead of verifying the prediction of Jules Lemaitre, that the last dove would be offered on the altar of the Muses, may more likely see the coming of a poet to be placed in the list of Homer, Virgil, Dante and Shakespeare.